A Road Taken

foreword by **Jean Chrétien**

A Road Taken

My Journey from a CN Station
House to the CN Boardroom

GREYSTONE BOOKS
Vancouver/Berkeley

Greystone Books Ltd.
www.greystonebooks.com

Cataloguing data available from Library and Archives Canada
ISBN 978-1-77164-066-4 (cloth)
ISBN 978-1-77164-068-8 (epub)

Copy editing by Shirarose Wilensky
Jacket and text design by Jessica Sullivan
Jacket photograph by John Hollander
Photographs courtesy of CN and McLean family archives
Printed and bound in Canada by Friesens
Distributed in the U.S. by Publishers Group West

We gratefully acknowledge the financial support of the Canada Council for
the Arts, the British Columbia Arts Council, the Province of British Columbia
through the Book Publishing Tax Credit, and the Government of Canada
through the Canada Book Fund for our publishing activities.

Greystone Books is committed to reducing the consumption of old-growth
forests in the books it publishes. This book is one step towards that goal.

to Brenda

Contents

Foreword

I MET DAVID MCLEAN in the summer of 1967, when a mutual acquaintance asked for a volunteer to pick me up at the Edmonton train station. I was minister of state for finance under the Honourable Mitchell Sharp, who was minister of finance. My chauffeur was David McLean, a young lawyer in his late twenties with an interest in public service and Liberal politics. It was Canada's centennial year, and I was travelling through western Canada by train with my family for meetings and other events to get a better understanding of that part of our vast country.

The mood of the country was positive and upbeat that summer, and there was an atmosphere of celebration in Canadian values that came, in part, from the energy of its young people. David McLean was one of those young people, so a year later, I offered him a job in Ottawa. But he had made a decision to move to Vancouver, where he would pursue a career in law and business. He would be very successful in both areas, and although he would never run for political office, he would give generously of his time and experience to countless business, academic, and community-service organizations in the private sector. We stayed in touch and met frequently at political and business events in Ottawa and elsewhere, and I came to know him as a respected Canadian business leader and a trusted friend.

Twenty-six years after our first meeting, I was elected prime minister of Canada. It was 1993 and the optimism of Canada's centennial year had taken a temporary back seat to a debt crisis that threatened the country's economic stability. Our priority was to eliminate the deficit and do what was necessary to balance the budget and restore Canada's fiscal reputation. This would include the sale of assets no longer best run by the government. One of those assets was the Canadian National Railway.

To succeed, we needed experienced people from the public and private sectors who understood the railway business and the long-term potential of CN's economic value to Canada. In looking for candidates from the private sector, David McLean's name was prominent. He had deep family ties to CN that were unique and long-standing, and he had a very clear vision of what needed to be done. He had also served as a director on the CN board when it was a Crown corporation, so he knew the challenges of the work that lay ahead. I had confidence in his judgement, and when he rejoined the board in 1994 and was elected chair a few months later, I knew we had a strong non-executive chair in place.

Eleven months later, the government of Canada completed the largest initial public offering of stock in Canadian history at that time. This, despite a referendum on the future of Quebec held a month before the IPO. David McLean's account of those eleven months, and the years that followed, makes for excellent reading and is an indication of why he has been annually reelected chair of the CN board an unprecedented nineteen times. Not only has CN remained a strong Canadian company headquartered in Montreal, it has successfully penetrated the U.S. market and become one of the world's greatest railways. I am proud of its success as a private enterprise company and grateful to David McLean for his unwavering commitment to the railroad his father once served as union steward.

They say a good memoir is a truthful and interesting account of the life and times of its author, but some say too much and some say too little. David McLean's book strikes the right balance in the right areas and is a lot like him—direct, engaging, and generous in sharing what has been important to him and what will be of value to the reader. He is a natural storyteller, but behind his stories of CN, law, and a family business is a message of perseverance and hard work.

Mostly, though, it is the honesty of his reflections on the role that family, sports, school, summer jobs, and spirituality have played in his success that separates his book from traditional business memoirs. This book is a very positive and insightful look at leadership from a great Canadian of energy, heart, and common sense.

The Right Honourable Jean Chrétien, P.C., C.C., O.M., LL.D.
PRIME MINISTER OF CANADA
1993-2003

"I shall be telling this with a sigh
Somewhere ages and ages hence:
Two roads diverged in a wood, and I—
I took the one less traveled by,
And that has made all the difference."
ROBERT FROST, "The Road Not Taken"

Preface

WHEN I SET OUT to write a memoir, I thought it would be about business leadership, with a few personal stories thrown in to keep the reader awake. It was a subject that interested me, and during the course of my life I had learned a few things about it. On paper, I had hit many of the marks. A prairie childhood and a passion for sports had translated into a legal practice, a family business, four honorary doctorates of law, decades of community service, and a thirty-year seat on the board of the greatest railroad in the world. And there were other achievements—other opportunities to develop and hone my interest in leadership.

I had chaired multiple boards and spearheaded international fundraisers for education, conservation, and health care. I had bought, built, restored, saved, and sold buildings in Alberta, Ontario, British Columbia, Hawaii, Georgia, California, and Arizona. I had won awards and travelled the world in a degree of comfort far removed from the modest means of my youth. I had campaigned hard for politicians I believed in and seen some fine candidates win and lose and sometimes win again. I had made friends with people from all walks of life and benefited greatly from their experiences and insights. And I had felt a knife or two in the back on occasion but nothing that pierced my soul or my conscience.

Law gave way to real estate, film studios, and aviation companies, and I learned the hard way that timing is not everything—health is—health in ways we don't always see or understand. My biography grew longer with the passage of time, the early struggles for cash gave way to wealth, and with that wealth, came the means to help others. A family foundation was established and the real power of money was revealed to me. Along the way, I found the right partner and we took the vow—in sickness and in health. We raised two sons who brought two wonderful daughters-in-law into our lives. We welcomed grandchildren into the world and felt the wonder of life through younger eyes again.

Through it all ran a connection to a railroad incorporated from a series of bankrupt railways on June 6, 1919. It was an event that took place about ten years after my father, Frank McLean, left grade school following the death of his parents. My father never talked much about losing his parents, but I know that he and his siblings—an older brother and two younger sisters—were taken in by their uncle Dan. Dan was a logger, and a rough customer by all accounts, but he owned a small house in Calgary's cold north end and gave them a roof over their heads. There would be no more school, though. They would have to earn their keep.

Dad was still a boy, but with grade five under his belt, he could read, think for himself, and more importantly, he seemed to have an ability to make decisions. With trains whistling through town day in and day out throughout his childhood, he must have decided at some point that a job with a railroad was a way of doing well in the world. His subsequent journey from grade school dropout to CN union leader would reveal his determination and shape the future of our family. Looking back, I don't recall him talking much about leadership, but I wonder now, more than a century after his birth, if he was more of a leader than he realized.

Brenda, my wife and partner in all things, says I have always tried to get from Point A to Point B in a straight line. It is a characteristic shared by many railroaders. But in writing my memoir, I have decided *not* to write a book that traverses neatly from Point A to Point B or focusses exclusively on the business of business. Instead, I have tried to tell an honest story about a prairie childhood, an education fuelled by team sports and ambition, a life in law and business, the family who mean so much to me, and a railroad.

These are the areas of my life that have taught me what leadership of any kind is really all about. It is a road I have taken and a journey I have loved.

"Yet there isn't a train
I wouldn't take,
No matter where it's going."
EDNA ST. VINCENT MILLAY

Introduction

MENTION TRAINS AND EVERYONE has a story to tell. It might be one of their own, or it might be a story told to them by others. Fact or fiction, they'll tell you their grandparents met on a train or a brother left home on a train. They'll tell you the train ran past an uncle's farm or along the river next to their hometown. They'll talk about the significance of trains in movies, books, song, and history. Mention trains and you'll get a response. Wave at an engineer on a passing train and you'll get a wave back. Trains are connectors. Passenger or freight, they power into the night and across the continent. The sight of a train makes us turn our heads, but the sound of a train tugs at our hearts and releases memory and emotion.

Everyone has a train story.

It was less than a month after the Quebec referendum. Many Canadians were still reeling from the narrowness of a vote that almost split the country, but I had played too many overtime games as a student athlete to worry about the distinction between winning and barely winning. A win was a win, and Canada was still one country. I was deeply grateful the separatists had not prevailed, but I had other things on my mind that night. It was just after seven o'clock in the evening in Montreal and I was sitting in the CN boardroom with a group of distinguished business leaders.

After eleven exhausting and exhilarating months, ownership of the oldest Crown corporation in Canada was about to change hands. It was the night before the initial public offering, or IPO, and we were nine times oversubscribed. It seemed the naysayers were wrong. Everyone wanted a piece of CN. Now it was up to the registered dealers to allocate the stock in accordance with the numbers presented to the Prime Minister's Office and endorsed by the minister of finance: 40 percent would go to Canadian institutions; 40 percent to foreign institutions; and the remaining 20 percent to the Canadian retail market. Not everyone agreed with those numbers, but I did, and as chairman, I had made my views known.

Who could have imagined that at age fifty-seven, I would be chairman of the CN board on this historic night? I was the son of a CN union steward, a man who never made it to grade six. My early years were spent in a prairie station house where the sound of trains and Morse code were the language of bedtime stories. Then again, I had built a foundation for just such an opportunity, brick by brick. I had a solid background in academics and sports, a lifelong interest in politics, degrees in arts and law, and a business career that enabled me to understand profit and loss—and know the difference. I had also served previously as a CN director. It was an eight-year appointment that began in 1979 during the Trudeau government, and although I learned much about the challenges facing CN as a Crown corporation, there were no signs of privatization when I left in 1986. All of these experiences had prepared me, and I could not have dreamt of a better challenge than the IPO. Like everyone else, I pushed myself hard in the months leading up to it, pushed my ideas, pushed my colleagues, and on more than one occasion, I was pushed right back. I loved every minute of it.

Those occasions were part of the process, but the atmosphere in the room that night was one of respect and celebration. Disagreements were no longer important. We had all been part of an internationally scrutinized business challenge, but our roles in meeting that challenge were different, and we were keenly aware of where one person's role ended and someone else's began. I was pleased, though, that all of the board members were present, because we had worked hard to create a board chemistry that could sustain the responsibilities of our agenda. We were united in our purpose to create solid shareholder value for all those who invested in CN stock, whether it was a large block that night or a single share next week. So as the registered dealers proceeded to allocate the oversubscribed stock, they did so with a sense of responsibility and fairness.

We were looking over the order book when I saw the name of a well-known Vancouver institution. I recalled a statement their CEO had made in the *Globe and Mail* a few months earlier. The *Globe*'s business editors had been asking money managers what they thought of CN going public. Most wished to remain anonymous.

"I wouldn't touch it with a ten-foot pole," said the CEO from Vancouver.

I took umbrage at this, so I called a broker I knew in Vancouver and asked if he knew who made the statement. The answer was affirmative.

"Well, call him," I said, "and ask if he would like to come to one of the CN information sessions in October. Tell him the underwriters have put together a road show he won't want to miss."

Flash forward to November 27 and there was the name of the financial institution in the order book.

"I guess they bought a twenty-foot pole," I said, "because this is a huge order."

Of course, because of the oversubscription, all of the orders got cut back that night, but everyone was treated fairly, including the pole-vaulting CEO from Vancouver, whose institution went on to become one of CN's top ten shareholders.

Things were proceeding in an orderly fashion when we received a phone call from Moya Greene. Moya was assistant deputy minister, policy and coordination, with the Department of Transport. She had a problem-solving mindset and had done an admirable job coordinating appropriate communications between the government and our executive team. The minister of transport, Doug Young, was on a business trip to China and had asked Moya to relay a few final details on his behalf. This included a request that everywhere David McLean was listed as chairman in the prospectus, the word "acting" be inserted to precede the word "chairman." It was late in the day for a change to the prospectus, but technically the minister was correct. I was not chairman but acting chairman.

The title accorded me had been adjusted because at the time of my appointment, eleven months earlier, CN was still a Crown corporation. Under the CN Act, the chair of CN had to be an order-in-council appointment, which meant the chair had to put all of their business interests in a blind trust. I wanted no part of that arrangement, so it was agreed that I would be called acting chairman of CN during its transition from a Crown corporation to an investor-owned company. In the aftermath of the IPO, it would be up to the board to elect a new chair at their discretion and at the appropriate time.

The phone call with Moya ended and everyone adjourned for a short break, but a few minutes later, a group of directors asked to speak with me in private. We went into an empty office and Cedric Ritchie, retired chairman and CEO of Scotiabank (then known as the Bank of Nova Scotia), acted as spokesperson for the group. The request from the minister had focussed their attention on who *should* be chair of the newly privatized company the next day. I was expecting a discussion and perhaps an overview of what CN would need in terms of board leadership as a private company. We had an extremely talented board, and I was open to all candidates for the position.

"We want you to be our chairman tomorrow and into the future," he said.

"Do the other directors feel the same way?" I asked.

"We're in agreement," he replied.

I thought for a moment (not too long in case they came to their senses) and said all right, but on two conditions. First, that my term be year to year and second, that I be evaluated by the board every year before standing for reelection. "To chair a board like CN," I said, "the chair needs the full confidence of the board."

When we rejoined the meeting, a resolution was moved, seconded, and unanimously approved that when the IPO closed the next day, I would be chairman of CN. It was a vote of trust in my leadership from a group of men and women I admired, and I resolved to justify that trust for however long I held the position.

JANUARY 2014 | VANCOUVER

Looking back on the success of the IPO, I see a number of elements that made it work.

First, we had a supportive federal government, headed by Prime Minister Jean Chrétien, who enjoyed the full confidence of his cabinet and made the critical decision to proceed with the IPO. His finance minister, Paul Martin, was an experienced businessman whose background in public and private sectors added depth to discussions that drove good decisions. And his transport minister, Doug Young, was a fierce advocate of the IPO who was protective of the government's interests and generous in sharing his views with others.

We had the right CEO in Paul Tellier, who worked extremely hard on cost cutting measures that prepared the company for privatization. It was no easy task. Others had tried, and some progress had been made, but Paul got the job done. We took a $1 billion write-down to cover severance for the eleven thousand people who were let go before the IPO. The financial and investment community (generally referred to as "the street") was supportive of this unpleasant but necessary decision because it saved more than $500 million per year in operating costs and made the company much more efficient. In human terms, we had to let eleven thousand people go to save the remaining twenty thousand jobs.

We had strong senior executives in Michael Sabia (then senior VP of corporate development) and Claude Mongeau (then VP of financial and strategic planning), who applied their experience, intelligence, and self-discipline to a workload of complex tasks few could master.

We had the CN pension fund, which was fully funded and exceptionally well managed by Tullio Cedraschi, who was president and CEO of the CN Investment Division. The board made a policy decision not to use CN pension funds to buy CN stock at the time of the IPO, or at any time thereafter, which calmed pensioner concerns as we approached the IPO. It was and remains one of the best managed pension funds in Canada.

We chose the right lead broker in the United States— Goldman Sachs. They were highly respected by the international community and their rail analyst, Craig Kloner, and point man on the deal, Mark Tercek, were outstanding. They understood that our intention was to create the most profitable and efficient railroad in North America.

We had a technically sophisticated road show, led by Paul Tellier and produced by an international production company called Imagination, that demonstrated the viability of the IPO and the strength of CN's executive team. It was, as Michael Sabia said later, "the best damned road show in the whole damned world." In my non-executive role, I was not part of it, but let me assure you, if there was an Academy Award for best dramatic adaptation of a prospectus, CN would have won it that year and Paul Tellier would have made the acceptance speech in two languages, flanked by Michael Sabia and Jack McBain (then senior VP of operations) on one side and the underwriters on the other.

We had access to excellent advisors, including Edward C. Lumley. Ed was a Liberal cabinet minister under two prime ministers—Pierre Trudeau and John Turner—but at the time of the IPO, he had left political life and was vice-chair of BMO Nesbitt Burns. There were few people more gifted than Ed Lumley when it came to steering strong-minded personalities away from unproductive conflict. He was an example of civility and intelligence to all of us.

We had one of the best business boards in North America, whose directors understood that a board has to act in the best interest of the company no matter who owns it. Their wisdom during CN's transition from Crown corporation to investor-owned company set the bar for future boards.

Finally, we had CN. No matter where we came from or what we did for a living or where we stood politically or at what level we were involved with the IPO, CN was the common denominator. It was a brand we all wanted to protect and enhance. In the midst of all the complexities and details leading up to the IPO, there was a certain simplicity in that. Somehow, the sheer weight of CN itself kept egos in check and responsibility on the table.

It has now been almost twenty years since the night of the IPO and I have been reelected chairman nineteen times. From this unique vantage point, I have seen CN transition from a struggling Crown corporation, openly ridiculed as "a pig with lipstick," to the most efficient, well managed railway in North America. I have seen market capitalization increase from $2.3 billion on the night of the IPO to about $50 billion today—a growth of more than 2,600 percent in less than two decades. I have seen strong executive teams push for efficiency—moving the operating ratio down and setting targets for management cost cutting, net revenue generation, return on capital, return on equity, and free cash flow, which are the concepts that have made CN the envy of the world in the transportation business.

And I have seen, in my own life, that among the bricks in the foundation that prepared me for a challenge like the IPO and the subsequent opportunity to chair the CN board for so many years, were bricks from other sources—ones that seemed unimportant to me at the time but valuable beyond all measure later on.

PART ONE

The Early Years

1

"A leader is a dealer in hope."

NAPOLEON BONAPARTE

Leadership

IN THE MIDDLE of his career at CN, my father was elected union leader with the Order of Railroad Telegraphers. For the next fifteen years, he would faithfully travel to St. Louis, Missouri, where the order was headquartered and meetings were held. He and his fellow telegraphers would discuss the issues of the day, the most important of which being how to improve labour relations at CN. It was an orderly business with a clear agenda for the most part, but on November 21, 1950, shortly after ten thirty in the morning, two trains collided at Canoe River, British Columbia.

The westbound train was a troop train carrying Canadian soldiers. Most were newly minted privates—young gunners with the 2nd Field Regiment of the Royal Canadian Horse Artillery—but some were veterans of World War II. They were all on their way to Fort Lewis, Washington, where they would be transported by military ship to Korea.

Half of the cars of the westbound train were wooden with steel frames.

The eastbound train was a passenger train less than a day into its transcontinental journey from Vancouver to Montreal. All of those cars were steel.

They collided on the turn at a blind corner a few kilometres south of the junction at Red Pass. The engineers and firemen of both trains were killed on impact. There was no loss of civilian life on the passenger train, but the wooden front cars of the troop train were devastated. Seventeen soldiers died, and many more were terribly injured—scalded by the steam from the damaged engine boilers.

The accident occurred in a remote high mountain area west of Valemount, British Columbia, and it took several hours before a train arrived from Jasper to take the survivors and casualties back to Edmonton. A second train was dispatched from Kamloops to pull the transcontinental train out of the area. It started to snow and the temperature dropped below freezing.

In the waiting hours, there were acts of bravery and resilience. Communications were down, but someone set up a temporary means of communication and put the emergency call in to Jasper. A doctor from the passenger train administered to the injured with the help of his wife, who was a nurse, and other volunteers. A hospital unit was set up in one of the dining cars and a morgue in the other.

My father was fifty-two years old, and I was twelve. We were living in Edmonton at the time, and I had just started junior high school. Dad must have come home early that day, because I remember him getting into his car and leaving shortly after I got home from school. He was worried that a lynch mob was going to hang the young operator everyone blamed for the tragedy. People were that upset. The operator was a twenty-two-year-old man named John Atherton stationed in a small town near the site of the accident. According to reports, he had omitted the words "at Cedarside" from a telegram delivered to the troop train at Red Pass Junction. The troop train was supposed to wait at a siding at Cedarside before proceeding west. Instead, the troop train carried on to Canoe River, unaware of the eastbound train.

Dad drove all night—first to the Interior where he picked up John Atherton, and then straight through to Vancouver where he thought the young man would be safer. I don't know if Dad thought his operator was guilty or innocent that night, but he wasn't going to abandon a man on his watch. I found out later that he took some of his vacation time to stay in Vancouver for a few extra days to ensure the operator was not harmed. But the story doesn't end there.

John Atherton was charged with manslaughter on January 9, 1951, but a Canadian lawyer named John Diefenbaker defended him at the request of his wife, Edna Diefenbaker, who was suffering from leukemia. John Diefenbaker was also the Member of Parliament for his home riding of Saskatchewan, and among his constituents was John Atherton's father, Alfred Atherton, a CN station master.

Alfred asked Diefenbaker to act as his son's defence lawyer, but Diefenbaker declined; he was too busy with his parliamentary obligations, he was not a member of the bar in British Columbia, and his wife was dying in a Saskatoon hospital. Determined, Alfred went directly to Edna, somehow gaining access to her hospital room. She listened to Alfred's story and promptly accepted the case on her husband's behalf. Diefenbaker would have to take and pass the B.C. bar exam first, however, which was said to be difficult and came with a steep $1,500 registration fee. Deferring to her judgement, Diefenbaker took the case. Edna died a few weeks later, on February 7, 1951. It was a month before the preliminary hearing.

In preparation for the hearing and the trial that followed, Diefenbaker researched and, in fact, studied telegraphy in an attempt to understand how words could be eliminated, interrupted, or overlooked in a message transmitted by wire. Among his findings was an account of transmissions being interrupted by a bird dropping a fish on a snow-covered wire.

"It was," he wrote later in his memoir, "not well documented, but it was all we had."

He was also determined to focus on other factors contributing to the tragedy, which included a need for block signalling, a sharp curve along that particular section of the line, a sequence of communications issues, and most importantly, the need to eliminate wooden passenger cars.

The trial lasted four days, and after forty minutes of deliberation, the jury acquitted John Atherton of all charges. Witnesses said his mother broke down and cried when she heard the verdict. John Diefenbaker, who would be elected prime minister of Canada in 1957, later wrote about the case in his book, *One Canada*. It was a defining moment in a distinguished career.

This brings me back to the subject of leadership. It seems to me that leadership is a term often misunderstood. People think of leaders as people who are popular and widely known. They think of politicians, community leaders, sports figures, academics, and business or professional leaders. These are all types of leaders in their own way, but in my view, the definition of leadership is not always tied to your position in life or even your responsibilities. It is certainly not tied to wealth. A true leader is a person who does the right thing when faced with a tough decision and who knows how to motivate others to follow their lead.

I see many examples of that type of leadership in the Canoe River tragedy: a doctor, a nurse, and a group of civilian volunteers working together under terrible circumstances; a father determined to get his son the best lawyer he could find; a dying woman who cared about the fate of a stranger in her last month of life; a railroad that adopted virtually every recommendation made to them to avert similar disasters; a future Canadian prime minister; and my father, Frank Carl McLean.

Dad was a man of quiet wisdom and compassion, and although I am often asked whether he would be proud of my service to CN as chairman of the board, I know it would not come close to the pride I felt for him that night in 1950.

IT IS 1952, *two years after the Canoe River train wreck, and I am running for junior class president. My campaign is going well and I anticipate an easy victory. My opponents are disorganized and distracted by their social lives, which are busier than mine. I use this to my advantage and win. It is my first taste of leadership and I like the experience, so a few years later, I run for senior class president against a friend. I lose. He wins. I am silently critical of his performance as president and believe for many years longer than I care to admit that I would have been the better leader. I am comforted somewhat when I am elected class valedictorian, but as time passes, I don't remember a single word of what I said in my address. I remember, though, that I lost an election and a friend won and that it took me a long time to understand what mattered and what did not.*

2

"Home is the seminary
of all other institutions."
E.H. CHAPIN

Home

WHEN I WAS BORN, home was the CN station house in Beiseker, Alberta. Dad was the station agent and my mother was a housewife. Together they created a home for their children, which, in my case, began with a drive by dirt road to Calgary on June 25, 1938.

Agnes Campbell, my mother, was in her mid-forties and she wasn't taking any chances. She had already suffered several miscarriages and lost three living children to the kinds of early childhood diseases that today are kept in line by vaccinations and antibiotics. She told my father that she didn't want to write "Beiseker" on the birth certificate. She wanted the baby to be born in a big city at a big hospital, and that meant Calgary, a two-hour drive by dirt road. You don't argue with a woman who is in labour for the sixth time.

Dad got the car and away they went. It was lucky they did, because I weighed almost thirteen pounds, which left my mother in need of hospital care for several days following my birth. Looking back, it seems likely she was a victim of gestational diabetes, which went largely unnoticed and untreated in older mothers in those days. Whatever the case, I confess to being grateful to her as a teenager and as a young man, not just for my safe arrival but because my birth certificate said "Calgary" instead of "Beiseker." "Calgary" sounded more important to me than "Beiseker," but perhaps that says more about me than Beiseker.

It was a very small town midway between Calgary and Drumheller, surrounded by rich grain-growing farmland. The Canadian Pacific Railway had put a branch line through in 1910, which was followed by a second line built by the Grand Trunk Pacific Railway in 1912. Roads were going in and settlers from the Dakotas were arriving with hopes that the area would become a major agricultural centre. It was not a world of water or tall trees, mountains or warm winters, but it was a safe world, and my parents moved there in 1922 with plans for the future. The Grand Trunk Pacific Railway had just been incorporated into the CN system and Dad was offered the job of CN station agent at Beiseker. The job came with a small house—a house they hoped to fill up as quickly as possible.

There was a kitchen, a living room, and a small study on the main floor, which connected to the train station's ticket office and waiting room. There were two small bedrooms upstairs and a root cellar under the kitchen to store food and other items. There was no electricity and no running water. Light came from kerosene lamps, and heat came from wood and coal until 1931, when the station was hooked up to power supplied by Calgary Power and a furnace could be installed. Indoor plumbing never reached the station house during my family's time in Beiseker, and my father carried buckets of drinking water from a well a block away from the station.

I LIKE TO say that Dad's railroad career began with a job delivering telegrams for the wrong railroad, but it was really his determination to learn Morse code that turned him into a railroader. He was just a young teenager when he saw an advertisement in a local newspaper for a night course on telegraphy and, by then, had upgraded his day job as a telegram delivery boy for the CPR to an errand boy at R.B. Bennett's Calgary law firm. R.B. would later leave the practice of law for a political career and go on to serve as the eleventh prime minister of Canada, presiding over a Tory government from 1930 to 1935. But in those days, the Right Honourable Richard Bedford Bennett was the founding partner of the most important law firm in town, and my father was the errand boy.

Dad signed up for the course and practised the code at night and in his spare time. And when he knew his dots from his dashes and his dits from his dahs, he was hired as a junior operator with the CPR. His switch to the right side of the tracks came a few years later, when CN offered him the job in Beiseker.

During the course of his long career with CN, Dad worked shifts as a train dispatcher. This meant I did not see him much, except on his days off, which were rarely on a weekend. So although we enjoyed a good relationship, I got to know him best when we took summer vacations by car to Vancouver, camping on the way. He rarely, if ever, attended my sports games or other activities, because he was usually working, but I always had what I needed to compete. I never went without. He was a hard-working, very loyal employee, who never had any debt and always paid his bills on time. I found a little book after he died with years of income and expenses carefully tallied in his precise handwriting. He wanted to make sure his accounts balanced, and they did. He was determined to live a quality life, though, and enjoy the things he could, such as buying a car that was just a little better than the base model. He appreciated having the best things he could afford, a characteristic he passed on to me.

Dad officially joined CN in April 1922 and remained with them in Beiseker, and then Edmonton, until he retired in 1963. He would live another thirty years, marry a second time, and move to Vancouver, Cranbrook, Victoria, and finally Vancouver again, where he would die in 1994 at the respectable age of ninety-five. But I'm getting ahead of myself. He hasn't met my mother yet, and neither have you.

MY MOTHER HAD a tough start in life. She was one of twelve children raised in West Hartlepool, a port town on the east coast of England. I know very little about her mother, but I know that her father, my grandfather, was a hard-drinking man who failed to provide for his family. Mother was born in 1894, when economic and social conditions were especially tough in England, but she was a resourceful girl and at the age of seventeen left England with two of her sisters. They made their way to Calgary and immediately went to work cleaning houses. It was 1911 and Calgary was booming. The first Calgary Stampede was held a year later, and for a working-class English girl raised in poor and crowded circumstances in the cold damp of coastal England, Calgary must have been a shot of pure oxygen. Agnes Campbell never looked back, and when she met a good-looking telegrapher named Frank Carl McLean, she became a Canadian wife who would raise a Canadian family. My father was twenty-one and my mother was twenty-five.

Their first son, Campbell, was born shortly after their marriage, and his arrival was followed a year or so later by their daughter Florence. Healthy at birth, both children would die before they reached their second birthdays. It must have been heartbreaking. Then came a survivor, my sister Lois, who was born on November 14, 1924. Lois would live a long and eventful life until September 2008, when she passed away in Vancouver at the age of eighty-four. Lois's arrival was followed by the birth of another son, Harvey, but he, too, died in early childhood. Then came a long decade of miscarriages and disappointment, until August 25, 1935, when another daughter, Daphne, was born. Like Lois, Daphne was a survivor and a strong presence in my childhood. She lives in the Fraser Valley of British Columbia now, but I suspect, to her, I might always be the annoying baby brother who came late in the lives of her parents and turned the station house upside down.

Diphtheria, scarlet fever, measles, mumps, pneumonia, flu, and polio—those were the killers of the day, but the truth is that I don't know what specific illness killed my brothers, Campbell and Harvey, and my sister Florence. It was not something people talked about. Children got sick and they died and they were buried and more children came after. It was the way of the times, but it was not without pain. I do know, however, that when Florence died, my mother was on a train, and when the conductor discovered the baby was dead, he told my mother she would have to get off the train. They couldn't have a dead body on the train. So when they got to the next town, my mother and her baby were loaded onto a buckboard wagon and taken, presumably, to the nearest mortuary. I will never understand the coldness of the man who put my mother off the train that day, a dead baby in her arms and no one there to help her.

With Lois and Daphne healthy and growing up, life went on in Beiseker, Alberta until it became apparent to my parents, almost twenty years into their marriage, that another baby was on the way. I was what they called a change-of-life baby, which in 1938 was an announcement to the community that the honeymoon was not over for the middle-aged station master and his English wife. Despite the odds of the day and the tragedies of the past, I was born loud and large at the Holy Cross Hospital in Calgary. Mother proudly put "Calgary" on the birth certificate and, a week or so later, returned home to Beiseker with her sixth and last child, David George Alexander McLean. She didn't do things by half.

I loved my parents very much because they gave me and my sisters everything they were capable of, despite the struggles of their own childhoods and the limits of their formal education. They wanted the best for their children. That was never in doubt. They gave us life, love, and home and with those three potent things—opportunity.

IT IS OCTOBER 2012 and I am in the rose garden at my home in Vancouver, clipping the last blooms of the summer. "The last rose of summer," I say, which is the only line of the old poem that I can remember. I will take these roses to the office later and distribute them to the staff. I don't leave roses for the men. I am old-fashioned and think my senior finance officer would quit if I left a rose on his desk. I choose the best ones for Brenda and leave them in a silver vase on her desk.

This garden is very different from the gardens of my childhood. Those gardens were filled with all kinds of vegetables and fruits—carrots, beans, peas, lettuce, tomatoes, raspberries, rhubarb, and the hated parsnips and broad beans my mother insisted on growing. Those gardens were large and flat and occupied the sunniest corner of the yard at all of our homes, from the station house in Beiseker to the homes in Edmonton that came later. I remember the taste of the seedling carrots pulled from the ground and the fresh corn that took all summer to grow. Rhubarb was stewed slowly and baked in pies with thick crusts and white sugar.

My Vancouver garden is filled with trees and flowers, and our gardeners do the heavy lifting and planting. Brenda likes the trunks of the big cedar trees and sees in them more beauty than in the neat rows of annuals our gardeners plant, which are too manufactured for her *liking. I see her frowning at the begonias lined up next to the house, and I worry about them. Beyond the edge of the property, I see the ships in the Vancouver harbour and the mountains of the North Shore.*

I have lived in many houses and own several. I like houses. There is a desert house for sun and golf, a winter house for skiing and mountain life, and a lakeside house for fresh air and tranquility. But this is the house I love. This is the house I used to walk past when I was a lonely student at the University of British Columbia living in a nearby boarding house. It is a house Brenda and I never intended to buy, but when we strolled into an open house following an expensive renovation of our other house— the house around the corner—we were in agreement. We would have to sell our newly renovated house and buy this one. We would have to get the carpenters back in and the drawings done and the plans filed and start again. We had found the home where we would raise our family and live happily for all of the decades that lay ahead.

3

"There is always one moment
in childhood when the door
opens and lets the future in."
GRAHAM GREENE

Childhood

IN 1941, WE LEFT the village of Beiseker for the bright lights of
the big city. The war was in full swing and Edmonton, the
provincial capital, was strategically located on the polar
route to Europe. It had become a major base for the move-
ment of troops and equipment and a vital link in the supply chain to Europe. Dad's work as a railroader classified
him as an essential service provider under the Schedule
of Reserved Occupations, which was hurriedly drafted in
1938 to protect services critical to home security. Not only
was Dad exempt from military service; he was prohibited
from it. He was, however, reassigned by CN to Edmonton,
so it was goodbye to the station house and hello to indoor
plumbing.

We lived in a house near the airport, where thousands of
U.S. troops were stationed to service the planes and protect
the airport. I was only three and have few clear memories

of those early wartime years, but I do remember my mother's anxiety, and my own youthful excitement, during the blackout drills. The air raid sirens would sound and Mother and my older sisters would fly into action, shutting off all the lights and drawing the curtains. We would have to stay indoors and wait for the sirens to sound the all-clear. There was never an attack, of course, but there was apprehension that one could happen at any time, particularly after Pearl Harbor when anything seemed possible.

I also remember the sound of the airplanes flying overhead—many, many airplanes. They were an endless source of interest to me, and as the war went on and I grew a little more aware, I learned to distinguish them. Our house was only a block away from the runway fence, so if I couldn't be found playing near the house—where I was supposed to play—I was most likely on my way to the fence. Watching airplanes was my principal occupation, but unlike children my age in Europe and other parts of the world, I had nothing to fear from those airplanes.

Looking back, I realize that the war did not affect my life emotionally the way it did so many other Canadians, because I didn't have any young uncles, cousins, or other close male relatives directly involved in the war effort. Had my older brothers, Harvey and Campbell, lived, they would have been young men and life might have been quite different for our family with two sons in uniform. As it was, my personal experiences of the war were largely shaped by a sense of adventure and a fascination with my mother's activities.

My mother had little education but she loved to read and did her best to increase her knowledge of the world on her own terms. She also had a strong sense of what was right and what was not. Good behaviour was important to her, along with self-reliance and doing what your mother told you to do. I was weak in two of those areas. If there is a single phrase that rings through my childhood, it is the sound of my mother's no-nonsense English voice saying, "Just wait until I get you home!"

Fortunately for me, she was as easy to distract as she was to annoy, and nine times out of ten, she forgot what I had done wrong by the time we crossed the dreaded threshold of home.

Throughout the war, she was active in women's auxiliary groups at Robertson United Church and the Red Cross, where she met with other volunteers to produce the vast quantity of hand-crafted items needed to support Canada's war effort. Like other women of her generation, she was frugal and resourceful—not a great cook, perhaps, but when it came to knitting, she held her own. According to my older sister Lois, she taught two generations of girls to knit and held numerous knitting parties in our home. So in addition to the sound of air raid sirens and airplanes, I remember the sound of her knitting needles turning out the woolen neck warmers she called "dickies" for our soldiers overseas.

There were times, however, when the sacrifices endured by other families came home to me in a darker way. I remember several occasions involving my mother going to a neighbour's house to console a family who had just received news of a son's death in Europe. Mother's feelings were clear to me then and planted the seed in my child's mind that soldiers were brave and important people. That truth comes home to me every year on Remembrance Day, when we stop to reflect, pray, and give thanks to the men and women who have died for our freedom and our values. Not just those who died but those who serve. The lessons of childhood linger.

And there are other lessons.

SOMETIME ON TUESDAY, September 5, 1944, Anne Frank and her family arrived in Auschwitz but on my side of the world, in a country where neighbours and their children didn't disappear in the night, I was getting ready for school. I didn't know how lucky I was; nor did I understand there were reasons for war that went far beyond the sound of airplanes, sirens, and knitting needles. I only knew that I had reached the important age of six and my formal education was about to begin. How lucky I was indeed.

I remember my first day at H.A. Gray Elementary School. It was an imposing building of red bricks and Gothic turrets on a large piece of land at the corner of 121st Avenue and 103rd Street. I couldn't wait to get inside and have a look around. I didn't cling to my mother nor she to me. She was fifty years old and happy to see the back of me as I passed through the boys' entrance and into the school.

Built in 1913, the school was named after Henry Allen Gray, who was also known as the Cowboy Parson. The story goes that he wanted to be a cowboy, but his mother said absolutely not, so he turned to the cloth. Whatever the truth was, he started out as a rancher near Calgary and ended up as a provincial judge. Sometime in the middle of his career, he became the first Anglican bishop of

Edmonton and a school trustee. He also started Edmonton's first Boy Scout troop, an organization that would come to mean a great deal to me.

I was what used to be called an active child. Maybe today my temperament would be called attention deficit disorder, but I remember it as a youthful enthusiasm for life. On a side note, a few years ago, a doctor treating me for an unrelated ailment said she thought I might be dyslexic after noticing the way I wrote. Who knows? All I know is that if I was, or am, dyslexic, I never let it hold me back. But I digress—probably confirmation of my condition.

After what I thought was a good first week, my mother was called by the school, who said they would be putting me in a special class. In the vernacular of the day, this meant a class for those who were slow. My mother was mad. She was a fighter and she didn't have slow children. She was at the school as fast as she could get there and refused to agree to the "special class." After a few more tests, the school agreed and I was reinstated into the regular class. I have always been grateful that I had someone who loved me so much she would fight for me that hard. I can't imagine how tough it would have been for me to fight the stigma of the special class as a little boy. The education system was not as forgiving then as it is now.

That aside, elementary school was fun, but there were tough times. The use of the strap as a punishment for bad behaviour was still liberally applied, and at H.A. Gray, there were two of them—a black one for everyday infractions and a red one for greater sins. Teachers could strap a child with impunity, and once the decision had been made, punishment would be administered at the back of the class on an open hand within clear earshot of the rest of the class to serve as a warning. Many of us were strapped (gum chewing was a capital offence of which I was guilty on occasion), but I'm not sure it did any good, except to engender bitterness towards the teachers and the school. It was not just because of the physical pain but because of the humiliation. The best you could hope for was to get through it without crying, but not everybody did. Thankfully, these methods are no longer socially acceptable and we have discovered better ways to preserve order in the class than whipping a child's hand with a leather strap.

Despite the challenges of the classroom, I held my own, but it was on the school's playing field that I really excelled. The playing field unleashed my love of sports which gave me a healthy outlet for my prodigious energies. With no brothers of my own, sports put me in the company of boys my own age who, like me, understood the joy of a ball and a playing field and a minimum of adult supervision. Sports alleviated my loneliness as a much younger child with older parents. I happily played baseball, football, basketball, and hockey throughout my childhood, and when my mother signed me up for violin lessons, I quickly learned to ditch the violin under the wooden sidewalk and make a run for the baseball field. I never became a concert violinist, but I could really hit a baseball.

above My father, Frank McLean *(second from left)*, in a family photo taken shortly before his mother died.

above My parents, Agnes (née Campbell) and Frank McLean. They were good to each other and their children.

facing top left Christmas 1946 and bow ties were in fashion.

facing top right Graduation from the University of Alberta law school, May 1962.

bottom right The 1955–56 Alberta provincial high school champions. I am number 23 in the front row. Coach McIntosh is on the left.

above Brenda and me with our sons, Jason *(left)* and Sacha *(right)*, at our home in Vancouver.

top right My wife, Brenda.

bottom right Jason, Brenda, and Sacha on the night I was invested into the Council of Governors following my 1992–93 term as chair of the Vancouver Board of Trade. In 2010–11, Jason would serve as the youngest chair in the board's history and its first second-generation chair.

above Our first family wedding—Sacha and Melanie.

top right The best man (Jason) is on the left. The groom (Sacha) is on the right.

bottom right Our second family wedding—Jason and A.J. (Andrea Jane).

top Christmas 2013, and our family is growing.

above Prime Minister Jean Chrétien at the opening of The Land-ing, 1985.

4

"Be prepared."
SCOUT MOTTO

Youth

IT IS 1986 and I am forty-eight years old and a prime candidate for burnout. High interest rates have a choke hold on my real estate investments and I am practising law on the side. I am also chairman of the board of governors at the University of British Columbia and nearing the end of an eight-year appointment on the CN board. I love the railway business and am proud of my family's long association with CN, but I hate the way Crown corporations are governed. There is too much political interference for my taste. I am happily married and have two sons I see about twenty minutes a day. Jason is thirteen and Sacha is eleven. What will they remember about their father when they look back on these years? I resolve to take on no further obligations when my services to CN and the University of British Columbia come to a close. No more extracurricular commitments.

I will learn to say no. Brenda is in agreement. With two young sons in school, it is time for us to free up some unstructured family time.

The phone rings. It is the headmaster from St. George's School. He has some bad news. They are shutting down the Scout program at St. George's. My sons go to St. George's and they are both active Scouts. They love the program, as I did when I was a boy their age. Loved it so much, in fact, I went on to be a Queen's Scout and the leader of my Edmonton troop.

"Why?" I ask.

"The scoutmaster is leaving," he says. "We've lost our scoutmaster."

"We'll have to find a replacement," I say.

"Who?"

But I don't answer. I am remembering the great times I had at Scout camps and meetings when I was a boy. I am remembering a man named Henry Price White, who hosted the camps on land he owned east of Edmonton.

I met Henry when I was eight years old. He was my cubmaster and my scoutmaster, but he was much more than that. He was an Albertan of basic values who influenced thousands of young people to make the right decision at critical times in their lives. He was a good man who took pride in seeing his Scouts mature and succeed. It was Henry who taught me how to properly use a knife and an axe—skills of importance to me. I remember quitting Scouts when I got a chance to play competitive hockey and then changing my mind. I went to see Henry after school to ask him if I could come back. I didn't know what to do and was afraid to tell the hockey coach.

Henry told me that if you believe you have made the wrong choice about something, it is never too late to correct your course. He told me that we all need to learn from our mistakes. I summoned up the courage to quit hockey and return to Scouts. I learned different lessons there— lessons I wouldn't learn in school or on the playing field. I maintain a friendship with Henry long after my scouting years come to an end. I name my favourite dog after him. Henry gets a kick out of this when I tell him. He knows how much I love that dog.

"David?"

"Yes?"

"The scoutmaster, David? Do you have someone in mind?"

"Yes."

"Who?"

"Me!"

I hang up the phone. Oh God, how am I going to tell Brenda about this? And how will Sacha and Jason feel about their old man as scoutmaster?

SCOUTS IS AN organization that takes young boys from the age of ten to fourteen—a vulnerable time for many—and teaches them life skills that are so diverse, they are bound to find something they are really good at and enjoy doing. In my case, Scouts introduced me not only to a world of new skills but also to a love of the outdoors that I might not have experienced on my own. I wanted to share those experiences with my two sons and their friends. Scouts gave me a break from the classroom as a boy. Now it would give me a break from the boardroom as a man.

From 1986 until 1989, I ran the Scout program at St. George's School. My secretary would interrupt me every Thursday afternoon at three o'clock and I would stop whatever I was doing to put on my Scout uniform and join the boys. To them, getting their next badge was more important than a business meeting. For me, that perspective was equally important. It brought me back to basic values.

Inspired by Henry's camp, I created a similar camp on a forty-acre parcel of land Brenda and I owned on Bowen Island. It was a magical place, close enough to town that the boys could easily get there on a Friday evening for a camp-out over the weekend. There was plenty of room, so I designed a military-style ropes course that included a climbing wall at the end. I very much doubt it was to playground code, but none of the boys got hurt propelling themselves over the wall or landing on the other side.

Many of my Scouts were kids who had not made the rugby team, or any of the other teams, and some of them had limited life skills. More than a few of them had been parented by well-meaning mothers who focussed only on academics, so my challenge was to teach those boys a whole world of new life skills. I decided to start with knives and axes, but not everyone agreed with my approach.

I remember coming back to the school after our first camp to find a very alarmed mother waiting for me.

"My son says he has been using a knife and an axe this past weekend at your Scout camp," she said. "Don't you think that's dangerous?"

I said, "Well, maybe it would be for you, but not for your son because he is perfectly safe handling knives and axes because he knows what he's doing and understands Scout policy on the use, storage, and care of both items. And there's a merit badge in this," I added, "when he learns how to use a saw."

She was unconvinced—aghast, actually—but over the next few months, things settled down and on Parents' Day, when she and the other parents came to our Scout camp, I could see on their faces the pride they took in the life skills their sons were learning and the merit badges that went with them.

When I took over the troop, there was a boy of about twelve years old who had been in Scouts for two years and never been in a leadership position and never earned a merit badge. He was a boarder at St. George's and it was my understanding that his parents lived in Toronto. In truth, his mother had died a few months before school started and the boy had been devastated by the loss. But I didn't know that until later.

What I did know was that the boy I met at our weekly Scout meetings was very quiet and unsure of himself, and it didn't help matters that he was shaped like a pear. Maybe it was the cut of the pants, but I looked a bit like a pear myself in my scoutmaster's uniform. I couldn't do much about that, but I could do something to bolster the boy's confidence.

I asked Brenda to go to a sewing store and have them make up a badge with a big Q on the front of it. At the next Scout meeting, as we came to the end of our regular activities, I gathered the troop together and announced that I was going to award a very special badge that had never been awarded in our Scout troop before. I brought out the

Q badge and of course they all wondered what it meant and who it would go to. I said the Q stands for quartermaster. A quartermaster is responsible for the distribution of supplies and provisions to the troops.

"This badge will go to the individual responsible for organizing our equipment and ensuring we are properly prepared for all of our trips," I explained.

I then called up the pear-shaped boy, who was even more surprised than the rest of the boys, and said, "Congratulations. I am appointing you quartermaster of St. George's Scout troop."

I couldn't have asked for a better outcome. Our new quartermaster took the job very seriously and the following week approached me at a school event.

"Sir, I have checked all our equipment and we are ready to go this weekend," he said.

"Good," I said. "Well done."

True to his word, at camp that weekend he had all the boys lined up in the morning brushing their teeth and washing their hands, and then standing in an orderly line for breakfast. He was a natural. And at the end of the year, in a secret ballot for Scout of the Year, my quartermaster won the title hands down. This recognition—which came from his peers—changed his life. He went from a boy who was largely ignored and uninvolved to someone who was liked for who he was and respected for his leadership and service to the troop. His father called me from Toronto to express his gratitude for the award and for the change he saw in his son's confidence. I assured him the only thing I did was give his son a chance to prove himself.

"Perhaps," said his father, "but he will remember this for the rest of his life."

"Me too," I said.

Leadership takes many forms. It doesn't always have to be up front and showy. Sometimes it is just the subtle nudging of a person to make them believe in themselves at a critical time in their life.

IN MY LAST year as scoutmaster, we had twenty Scouts who achieved the Chief Scout's Award, the highest honour in Scouts. The boys worked hard and completed all of the requirements well before the year's end. Together, they made up the largest number of Chief Scout's Awards earned by one troop in the country. I thought of Henry White when I got the news.

I decided to celebrate and announced I would take the boys to the Canadian Scout Jamboree in Prince Edward Island. But instead of taking a direct flight, I decided to organize a slightly more elaborate sightseeing expedition. I was an experienced scoutmaster, after all, and what could be difficult about a trip across the country with twenty adolescent boys? Aside from the cost of feeding them—nothing.

First we went to Seattle, where we changed planes, then to Chicago, where we met with local Scouts and saw the city. Then we went to Halifax and Charlottetown, for the Jamboree, and on to Boston, where we met with more Scouts, toured the Kennedy Library and saw the beauty of Cape Cod.

When we arrived home, the look on their faces as they greeted their parents was ample reward for all the work of organizing the trip. They were a tired bunch of boys but filled with stories about where they had been and what they had seen. Of course, it helped that two of those boys were my own sons, Jason and Sacha, who had—I learned later—a few stories of their own about life on the road with Scoutmaster McLean.

I LOST MY hero in 1991. Henry was eighty-four years old and I had maintained contact with him for forty-four years because he had such a positive impact on my life. In 1988, I invited him to Vancouver to meet the St. George's Scouts. True to form, he was an inspiration to those pre-teen boys.

When Henry died, the *Edmonton Journal* published a tribute to him that ended with the following words: "Henry Price White left an indelible mark on the life of every person he met. He did more for the east-end youths than anyone of his time."

As one of those youths, I can attest to the veracity of that statement.

5

"You miss 100 percent of
the shots you don't take."
WAYNE GRETZKY

Scorecards

I WAS ALWAYS INTERESTED in sports. Perhaps it was because they enabled me to burn off excess energy and gave me an outlet for my competitive nature. Perhaps it was because I was bigger and stronger than most boys my age. Who knows? All I know is that I loved to play sports—almost any sport—from the moment I discovered the relationship between their existence and my own. Sports were something I understood better than other things in my life, and I was good at them. That went a very long way in building my confidence as a boy and tempering it as a teenager. I loved to win, but I learned early that losing was not as important as knowing there was another game next week. Learning to accept loss without bitterness or blame is, and always will be, one of life's great lessons.

The sports I played were tied to the seasons, which in a northern city like Edmonton changed quickly. The smell

49

of leaves piling up in the front yard—and tomato pickles cooking in my mother's kitchen—meant football. The smell of snow on a cold north wind meant frozen ice rinks and hockey. The smell of dirt and new grass meant baseball. No matter what the season, though, I was rarely without a bag of gear ready to go by the back door. The days in Edmonton were especially long in the summer, and by the time I was a teenager, I usually had a summer job that cut into my free time. But after work, there was always enough daylight left for a pickup game of something or the occasional trip to a public golf course for nine holes and a fight to the death with the local mosquitoes.

It must have baffled my parents, whose own childhood experiences of sports were non-existent, to have a son who ate, slept, and dreamt sports. They were tolerant and supportive, though, and gave me considerable freedom in choosing my own activities. When I was in elementary school, my favourite sport was baseball, but as I grew taller and started junior high school, I discovered basketball, which was and remains my passion. I played for our junior high school team in grade eight and we won more games than we lost, but win or lose, it was on the basketball court that I experienced the great joy of doing something I truly loved.

There were no facilities available to me outside of school, so to satisfy my twenty-four-seven appetite for basketball, I rigged up a hoop in our basement out of chicken wire with an orange sack for a net. I mounted my hoop on a six-by-eight-foot beam that ran across the basement ceiling but was only about six feet off the ground. I would spend hours in the basement using a tennis ball to do layups and shoot foul shots until I was tired out or called upstairs for supper. It may have been a simple set-up, but it was everything I needed to imagine I was in the NBA shooting the final shot in a critical game. This was the moment. Would I make the shot? Needless to say, the walls of my room were covered with magazine cut-outs of famous NBA players.

The summer I turned thirteen, Dad helped me mount a real hoop in the back of the garage, no doubt to reduce the sound of tennis balls ricocheting around the basement. There was not much room between the hoop and the garage, so layups were a problem, but I was able to shoot foul shots and long jumpers, which gave me great practice. With two hundred shots a day times sixty days of summer holidays, I couldn't help but improve, and when I returned to school that fall, I was elated to discover that I was more advanced than the other guys on the team. It made me realize the importance of practising your sport, even if your mother looks like she is ready to ship you off to Siberia on occasion.

It all paid off in high school when I made the junior team as a starter. I was a big scorer and rebounder, and I got a lot of school press that year, often scoring twenty-plus points in a game. I was on a winning team but already had my sights on the next level—the senior high school team, which was generally made up of boys in grade twelve. I would have to be exceptional to wear the jersey of the senior team as a younger student. It was back to the garage.

Then in grade eleven, it happened. I was called up to the senior team towards the end of their season. I mostly warmed the bench, but in the final game of the city championship, when one of our star shooters was injured in the last minute of play, the coach turned to me and said, "McLean, you're in."

McLean, you're in!

I was in shock, but my ambitious nature knew it was the opportunity I'd imagined. Knees knocking, I started to sweat. *Please, God*, I prayed, *please keep my hands dry.* The team took a time out and our coach, Don Macintosh (a brilliant young coach and athlete who would play for Canada at the Melbourne Olympics in 1956), called us over.

"All right," he said, "we have twenty seconds left and we're tied, so our best players will be closely guarded, but they may neglect McLean because they don't know him and won't expect him to shoot. I want you to move the ball around the outside and if none of you have a good shot and you can't clearly get it to our centre—pass it to McLean."

Pass it to McLean!

"McLean."

"Coach?"

"I want you to shoot if you're open."

I want you to shoot!

The game resumed. We threw the ball in and our veteran players passed around the outside, and the defending team proceeded to do just as our coach thought they might do. They played five on four and left me wide open. The clock ran down to five seconds and, suddenly, I had the ball.

I HAD THE BALL!

I had a fleeting flashback to all those long summer nights behind the garage, sinking long shots with nothing but net. Thousands upon thousands of long shots. Bounce, thud, bounce, bounce, thud, bang, thud, bounce. It's a wonder I wasn't arrested.

I put the ball up, and with just a second left, I scored—nothing but net.

It doesn't get much better than that for a sixteen-year-old boy. I knew it then, and I know it now. Truth be told, I can still make the shot in my mind if I'm alone with my dog, Henry, who seems to understand when I get that faraway look on my face. It is a look he shares when he sees a rabbit on our morning walk.

Mostly, though, I will never forget the celebration that followed our spectacular win as city champions. I went to bed that night knowing my position on the senior team had just been assured. "Pass it to McLean" were the best words of my young life.

My love of sports, however, had to take a back seat to the reality of summer jobs, because as much as I loved game time, a chronic shortage of cash could only be solved one way for me—by earning it myself.

I WAS FOURTEEN when a neighbour, an executive with a national drug company, asked my father if I would be interested in a summer job. I was big for my age, so he must have thought I was much older, but when Dad told me about the offer, I said, "Absolutely—what will I be doing?" Dad said I would be packing, shipping, and stocking drugs in the company's warehouse. A warehouse job! Boy, was I pumped! All my pals had paper routes at best and worked hard for paltry sums. But I would be a big guy—a warehouse worker. I couldn't wait to tell them.

The first day, I packed my lunch, jumped on my bike, and pedalled the eight kilometres to the warehouse, where I was handed a lab coat and directed to the shipping department. The other workers were mostly men in their late twenties to early fifties, but they must have thought I was older, too, because everyone was friendly and treated me like one of the guys. I quickly settled in to the routine of a working man. Clock in at eight, work a couple of hours, go for coffee, work a couple of hours, eat lunch, work a couple of hours, more coffee, work a couple of hours, clock out at five and—in my case—pedal home. The social centre of the warehouse was the lunchroom, which was run by the janitor, a white-haired man named Ted Woods who wore a janitor's smock. Ted made the coffee, kept the lunchroom clean, swept the warehouse floors, and cleaned the offices of the higher-ups. He was a nice man, but he wasn't one of the guys. The guys didn't wear smocks.

A few weeks into the job, the warehouse manager came to me and said, "Dave, Ted's going on holidays for three weeks and we want you to take over his job. He'll train you this week, and after that, you're on your own."

Train me? My delusions of grandeur were crushed. I was no longer a big guy on the warehouse floor. I was a janitor, or at least I would be—after I was trained.

I never said a word to anyone. I pedalled home that night, had dinner, and went upstairs to my room to think. On the one hand, I would have to be a janitor for three miserable weeks, which seemed like an eternity to me. On the other hand, I was getting paid well and if I quit, not only would I lose my income (which I badly needed), but I would be humiliated thanks to my own big mouth in telling all of my friends I was making triple their incomes. Money and pride were on the table and I wasn't sure then if you could have one without the other.

I became the janitor. For the next three weeks, I took a lot of ribbing from the other workers, who decided to call me Teddy. They would roll up their lunch bags and toss them my way saying, "Teddy, pick that up and keep this place clean, would you?"

I ignored them. I would be fifteen in a few weeks, and I might be wearing a janitor's smock now, but I wouldn't be wearing one forever because I was going to do well in school and have a big career—if my plans to play in the NBA fell through. But as I did the job, the thought slowly seeped into my adolescent mind that if I was going to be a janitor, I might as well be a good one. And as I swept floors and bagged the lunchroom garbage, my pride was mysteriously restored.

FOUR SUMMERS LATER and I was still sweeping.

It was my grade twelve year and I was finally in the kind of special class my mother liked. It was an honour roll class of twenty-five students who carried heavier than average academic loads and were expected to maintain high marks. We had been together since grade ten, and many of us had become good friends, but I was the only one who raced from the library to the football field. My classmates were all top students, but none of them shared my passion for sports or extracurricular activities that might cut into study time. But I thrived on a diversity of challenges, so in addition to football and the special class, I was also on the basketball team and the student's council, where I held the lofty title of chairman of Victoria Composite High School's athletic board. Later that year, I would be selected by the Rotary Club to represent Edmonton high school students at an annual Ottawa event called "An Adventure in Citizenship." Joe Clark, a future prime minister, would be among the other student delegates from Alberta.

I loved it all. I loved being busy and I loved the challenges. Hey, it was 1955! I could walk and chew gum. I had a brush cut that squared off the top of my head like a block of cement, and the great Jackie Parker (AKA Old Spaghetti Legs) was playing for the Edmonton Eskimos. If I kept my grades up and secured a little financial assistance, I would soon be a student at the University of Alberta. In the meantime, it was football season.

We had a great team that year, and three of our best players would go on to play for the Edmonton Eskimos. They were tough kids from the east side of town, but for some reason I never quite understood, they never had a towel. I was from the north end of town and we were far from well off, but at least I had a towel. When we hit the showers after practice, my towel would invariably be "borrowed" by the east-end guys.

"Dave, toss me the towel."

The towel?

But I knew if I valued my teeth, I would just have to wring it out and say nothing.

We had an undefeated year and won both the city and provincial championships. I was an end because I was six foot two and a master at catching short passes, especially when we needed a first down. Our tough and towel-less line blocked well, which made me look good, so with their help, I caught seven passes for first downs in the final game and we defeated our arch rivals, Crescent Heights High School from Calgary.

I took a few weeks off for Christmas exams, and then it was on to basketball.

Like the football team, our basketball team had a lot of talent, but it wasn't quite the championship material of my grade eleven team in terms of star players. We would have to work harder to succeed, but Coach Macintosh, who was now actively training for the summer Olympics, really understood the game from a strategic point of view. He taught me how to rebound and how to cause my check to foul me.

"You're going to be a role player," he said, "and a great rebounder, which means you're going to get fouled, which means you'll need to be a great foul shooter."

He would make all of us stay after practice and shoot foul shots until we had ten in a row. Some players were there for a long time, but it paid off and we rarely missed a foul shot in a game.

When spring came, we found ourselves, to our surprise, in the provincial championships. As luck would have it, we were up against our Calgary rivals, Crescent Heights again, who were still burning from our football win. To complicate matters further, Don Macintosh had a younger brother who played for Crescent Heights and averaged more than thirty points a game. I'm not sure how it played out at Macintosh family dinners in later years, but a few minutes before the game, Coach Macintosh took me aside and said, "McLean, you'll have a very special job to do in this game."

"What is it?"

"Get my brother fouled out as soon as possible."

I knew just what to do. I shadowed his brother like a ghost; every time a shot went up, I was right there between him and the ball. I would get the rebound, lean into him, and the referee would call a foul. By halftime, the poor kid had four fouls. One more and he was out of the game.

"Keep it up, McLean," Coach said at halftime, and it was on to the second half.

Two minutes into the second, his brother missed a shot and I snagged the rebound. I leaned into him and he was fouled out of the game for good. He had scored only ten points in a provincial championship and would now have to watch the rest of the game from the bench. I wish I could say I had mixed emotions, but I had done my job, and a few minutes later, we were up twenty points. Then came the lesson. Don Macintosh called a final time out.

"McLean, you did a great job," he said. "But I want you to sit out the rest of the game so I can give some of the other guys a chance to play."

To my surprise, I was okay with this decision. I had listened carefully and done what was asked of me, but it was time to share the glory with my teammates and perhaps feel a little of the pain of an opponent who, like me, was now sitting out the remaining minutes of a championship game.

We won by a wide margin.

AND THEN THE year was over. I was class valedictorian one day and warehouse janitor the next. It was not football, hockey, basketball, or baseball season anymore. It was just summer, and for the first time in my life, nothing about September was certain.

About a month after exams, my mother came to the warehouse and asked to see me. I came out of the lunchroom wearing my janitor's smock and she said a letter had arrived from the Department of Education. "It's your grade twelve marks," she said.

I opened the letter and, despite all the sports and extra-curricular activities, I had graduated with first-class honours. Mom was thrilled. She was always my biggest cheerleader. When she left, I stuffed the envelope into my smock and returned to the lunchroom, which was filling up with hungry warehouse workers. As I was getting the coffee ready, I leaned over and the envelope fell on the floor. I was so busy, I never noticed it. One of the men picked it up—he was a big, mouthy guy. He opened the envelope, read the contents, and his next words were, "Holy shit! You guys should see this. Teddy's a genius."

I made a grab for it, but it was too late. The letter was being passed around. The room went quiet and the mouthy guy said, "Good for you, Dave. You're going to make something of yourself. You've been a great worker here and you deserve a good life."

They all clapped and I was so embarrassed. They were good guys and I knew that none of them were going to university that year, or probably any other year, and that if I knew it—they knew it, too. I learned different lessons about leadership in that lunchroom. I learned that my decision to do an outstanding job no matter what I was asked to do, and not complain about it, had earned the respect of men twice my age with half my chances.

At the end of the summer, they all got together and bought me a gift. I said goodbye, hung up my smock, and pedalled home for supper. I was keenly aware of the opportunities that lay ahead for me and promised myself I would never waste those opportunities or take any of them for granted. The flame was lit.

6

"To find yourself,
think for yourself."
SOCRATES

Law School

I AM IN MY LAST YEAR of a bachelor of arts degree at the University of Alberta and I don't know what to do next. My options are law, medicine, and teaching. I am a good athlete and love sports, so I think I would be a good high school or college coach. In addition to school teams, I have played for two years on the University of Alberta Golden Bears basketball team, which has taught me a lot about coaching at higher levels. I see myself leading Canadian teams to victory. Coach McLean—a leader of champions! But I am not sure if that's all that I want to do with the rest of my life.

I have good marks in the sciences, so medicine is a possibility, but I know that the only reason I worked so hard to get those marks was so that I wouldn't have to take any more science courses. That doesn't sound like doctor material to me.

And law? Well, I don't know any lawyers. I have never met one. My family has never needed legal advice.

I decide to seek career advice from a counsellor at the university. She spends a lot of time helping me come to a decision but after a series of tests, states the obvious: "David, you are clearly more oriented to the social sciences than the physical sciences."

I decide to try for law. My marks are high enough for admission, and in the fall of 1959, I enter first-year law at the University of Alberta. I have no idea what to expect.

"MR. MCLEAN."

"Dr. Smith?"

"This is an example of the Edmonton/Vegreville principle, is it not?"

"Sir?"

"Remind us where Vegreville is, Mr. McLean."

"It's a small town."

"I ask for carrots and you bring me a cabbage. The question was where, Mr. McLean, not what."

"Vegreville is a small town eighty kilometres east of Edmonton."

"Correct. So when it is raining in Edmonton, it might not be raining in Vegreville, yes?"

"No, I mean, yes, it might not be raining in Vegreville."

"Which means?"

"Which means it is not raining unless it is raining."

"The Edmonton/Vegreville principle, Mr. McLean: things are not always the same. Legal principles are not cut and dried. There are grey areas. It might be raining in Edmonton but not in Vegreville, so the secret is to know what?

"What?"

"I'm asking you, Mr. McLean."

"Where the rain stops and starts?"

"Did you hear the music, everyone? That is the beautiful symphonic sound of a correct answer well articulated."

MY FIRST YEAR was unnerving. The faculty consisted of four full-time professors, but what they lacked in numbers they made up for in intimidation. In my case, this was easily achieved, because I had no idea what they were talking about. Fortunately, the approach to law at the University of Alberta focussed on the fundamentals. First-year courses were compulsory and included torts, constitutional law, property law, and contracts—a course that almost did me in.

Our professors expected us to read the assigned cases and come to class prepared to discuss the legal principles involved. I had been a Chief Scout, so I knew all about the importance of being prepared, but none of my merit badges had prepared me for the Socratic approach to learning at law school. It wasn't enough to know something. You had to know why you knew it and how it applied and when it mattered and what it implied, and when you figured all of that out, you had to learn how to deconstruct it before another law student did it for you.

Prepared or not, we all shook in our boots when we heard our name called, because our professors had a way of making us feel five inches high if we could not clearly elucidate the principles of the case under discussion. There was no running for cover when that happened. Like the leather strap of my grade school years, the only recourse was to keep quiet and take the punishment, which came not with a blow to the hand but with a heavy professorial sigh and an upwards glance at the ceiling. I think it is safe to say we were all intimidated by the process, but as the year went on and we gained confidence, we began to experience the benefit of being able to discuss and debate legal issues. It was how we learned.

Wilbur Fee Bowker, OC, LLM, LLD (Hon.), KC, was dean of law. He was a man of great character who loved to get us fired up over complex and contentious legal issues. Discussions in Dean Bowker's classes were often loud and always memorable. Like many of us, he was Alberta born and educated but he was just twenty-two years old when he graduated from law school at the University of Alberta. He then practised law for ten years with Milner and Steer until 1942, when he enlisted as a private in the army. After the war, he returned to Edmonton and, in 1948, was appointed dean of law at the age of thirty-eight. By the time I sat sweating in his classroom eleven years later, he had completed a master of laws degree at the University of Minnesota and a fellowship at Yale. I mention this because it speaks to the quality of men such as Dean Bowker and the influence they had on my generation. Those of us who were children or young teenagers during the war were caught between a generation of veterans and baby boomers. Unlike the boomers, the veterans kept their secrets, but we felt the weight of their experience and wanted to earn their respect.

Dr. Alexander Smith, QC, of the Edmonton/Vegreville principle, was a veteran of a different war. Scottish born, he had contracted polio as a teenager shortly before he was due to start classes at the University of Alberta. This may have delayed his start but not his determination. He returned to the university in 1936, graduated from law school in 1941, and went on to earn a master of laws and doctor of jurisprudence at Stanford University. Like Dean Bowker, Dr. Smith articled with George Steer of Milner and Steer in Edmonton but left the practice of law after the war to join the university's faculty as a full-time law professor.

Dr. Smith wore heavy braces on both legs, walked awkwardly, and usually taught us from the lectern, which he gripped dramatically with both hands. He was a brilliant legal scholar and a bear in the classroom, but in private discussions in his office, he was an understanding and compassionate man. He saw it as his duty to train us well so that we would truly grasp the basic principles on which the law was based. He had a wonderful command of language and many funny expressions that he used as a way of telling us we were dead wrong about something without humiliating us. In Dr. Smith's classroom, I learned the difference between carrots and cabbages. I also learned how to survive first-year contracts, a course I feared and disliked.

Apparently, I wasn't very good at it either. I stumbled through the Christmas exam in a complete fog, and when the results were posted, saw "30%" next to my name. My world was shattered—my dreams of being Clarence Darrow or Lord Denning dashed on the altar of Dr. Smith's first-year contracts Christmas exam. I was not used to failing, but I had such a strong aversion to quitting that I knew I would have to go see Dr. Smith if I was ever to have the courage to return to his class. The problem was that I truly feared Dr. Smith. He was one of those intellectually sharp teachers who seemed to know what you were thinking before you did. I entered his office in a cold sweat, but he couldn't have been nicer.

"Don't worry about the exam, old man," he said as I got up to leave. "You just guessed wrong seven out of ten times. You'll do fine on the final, and I fully expect you'll graduate at some point and become a good lawyer."

He was right. I guessed right eight out of ten times on the final exam and did graduate as he predicted, and I believe I was a good lawyer. Better because of Dr. Smith's teaching. He made me dig in, not just to survive the misery of first-year contracts but to get what he called the "first principles" of the law *right*. I am forever in his debt and although I later moved beyond the practice of law, the principles I learned in law school remain with me more than fifty years later. More than a brick in my foundation, they are the ethical cornerstone of my character and although I have not actively practised law for almost thirty years, I still use those principles in every facet of my business and personal life. I was blessed to have had professional mentors such as Alexander Smith and Wilbur Fee Bowker, and I will never forget them. They taught law not leadership, but for those of us in their classrooms, the lessons were inseparable.

IN THE FINAL half of our graduating year, we all knew we had to get articles with a law firm for a year in order to qualify for admission to the bar. But in the early 1960s, there were no bar admission courses and no help at all from the university or local law firms in getting those articles. We were on our own, which in my case was a problem because I had no connections with law firms and my marks buried me somewhere in the middle of the class. I approached firm after firm without success and, despite my optimistic nature, began to worry.

I was sitting in the law library one afternoon when I overheard a classmate say he'd received two offers but had just turned the first one down for a better one.

I put on my game face and said, with as much disinterest as I could muster, "Which firms?"

"Well, Firm A wanted me," he said, "but I've decided to go with Firm B."

I waited a few more minutes and when the coast was clear, casually strolled out of the library and ran like a bank robber to the nearest pay phone to call Firm A.

"Put me through to the lawyer in charge of articling students," I said, since I didn't actually know the name of the lawyer in charge. Fortunately, the receptionist didn't ask any questions and put the call through. The lawyer in charge took my call and I announced my availability as an articling student.

"This is quite a coincidence," he said. "We were just turned down an hour ago by another student. When can you come in for an interview?"

"Would thirty minutes be too soon?" I asked.

I got the job. My entrepreneurial skills were beginning to show!

I joined Firm A in the spring of 1962 and practised there until 1968, with a year off for a trip to Europe. I was a quick study and developed a roster of excellent clients, which helped me build a substantial real estate and mortgage practice. I also ventured briefly into criminal law, successfully defending a man charged with cheating at cards—an outcome that came as a surprise to the defendant, me, the firm, and everyone else associated with the case.

It was about a month after I had been called to the bar and I was at my desk when the phone rang. It was the receptionist.

"I have a client for you," she said. "He needs a lawyer for a criminal matter and you're the only one available."

I opened my door and in walked a slightly built French-Canadian man. He was a cross between Al Capone and the driver of the getaway car.

He sat down in my tiny office and proceeded to tell his story. He had been working for eighteen months in Fort McMurray, where the development of the Alberta oil sands was underway. In the evenings, most of the men played cards, because there was not much else to do. Many of them were earning big money, so the pots were often quite substantial, especially later in the evening. My client was part of a seven-man group of card sharks who had moved to Fort McMurray to help the workers part with their money. They worked in pairs, he explained, initially losing small pots of money, but as the pots grew, they began to win. They would move from table to table to alleviate any suspicion. They used cards that had been treated so that the hands could be read from the outside of the cards.

After a few months, the RCMP got wind of it and sent in an undercover squad to catch the card cheats. It took several months, but eventually they had enough evidence to arrest all seven members of the gang. Cheating at cards was a serious felony under the Canadian Criminal Code and the penalties for conviction were severe.

I told my client that I would have to attend a preliminary inquiry in Fort McMurray, followed by a trial in Edmonton, and that I would require a fee of $1,000 up front for the preliminary inquiry with an additional $4,000 up front for the trial.

He pulled out a wad of bills, counted out $1,000 and put them on my desk. This guy was serious!

I asked him why he came to "my firm" and he said he had a falling out with the other card sharks after the arrest and got cut out of their plans for a defence.

"What was the falling out about?" I asked.

"Money," he said.

The others had split into two groups of three. One group had retained Milt Harradence from Calgary. Milt was a brilliant and flamboyant criminal lawyer who flew around in an old World War II jet. The other group retained Gifford Main, a prominent criminal lawyer based in Edmonton.

My client said he wanted someone young and keen who would give him a good defence. Well, he was in luck, because I was green as grass. I asked him a lot of questions and took copious notes before I wrote him a receipt and bid him adieu.

I went to Fort McMurray a few weeks later for the preliminary inquiry. The other high-powered lawyers were in attendance, so I decided to sit back and listen to them ask questions and take notes. They asked all the right questions and I compiled extensive notes. It was clear that this was going to be a costly prosecution, as the Crown had eight undercover agents they would have to call as witnesses. They would also have to call experts on card cheating to explain how the accused had cheated, and these experts had to be brought in, at great expense, from Chicago.

I decided to keep a low profile and ask no questions. In fact, I slipped out a little before it was over to avoid drawing attention to my client.

When I got back to Edmonton, I called my client and explained what happened at the preliminary inquiry. I told him that it would be best if we kept a low profile and that he should not talk to anyone before the trial, which was now set for a few months down the road. I also asked for the balance of my fee, $4,000, which he promptly paid in cash.

On the day of the trial, I went to the courthouse with my client and sat in the back of the courtroom. The other lawyers sat in prominent positions at the front with their clients and the prosecutors.

The judge came in and we all stood. He asked the clerk to read the charges for the first accused who, fortunately for me, was not my client. After the charges were read, the prosecutor stood up and announced that they had agreed to reduce the charges to a lesser charge in exchange for a guilty plea. So each of the six accused stood up and agreed to plead guilty to a lesser charge and pay a hefty fine.

Finally, the prosecutor read the original charge to my client. I stood up and walked to the front of the courtroom and said we were pleading not guilty and we were ready to proceed with the trial. The prosecutor shot me a look of intense disapproval and asked for a short adjournment. He approached me with a smile that put me in mind of a grade school teacher who couldn't decide between the red strap and the black one.

"We have a deal to reduce the charges and *your client will plead guilty,*" he said evenly.

"You have made no such deal with me," I said, "and I am ready to proceed with the trial."

He was not amused.

When the judge returned, the prosecutor said he would stay (drop) the charges against my client. The judge agreed to stay the charges and told me that my client was free to go. I grabbed my client and got out of there as fast as my legs would carry me.

"Is it over?" my client asked.

"Yes!" I said.

I went back to the office and about an hour later the receptionist phoned me. "Your client's back," she said.

"Send him in," I said and opened my door.

"You did a great job for me," he said, "and I know I already paid your firm $5,000 for you to defend me, but I wanted you to have something more for yourself because you're just a junior lawyer, so here's a thousand bucks for you."

He then proceeded to place a large stack of twenty-dollar bills on my desk.

"I cannot take this," I said in my best lawyer voice. "Anything you pay me must go to our firm."

"It's cash," he said. "Just put it in your pocket. No one will be the wiser."

"I cannot do that, but I will add it to our fee if you agree."

"Look, it's for you," he said. "Do whatever you want."

I wrote him a receipt, thanked him for his business, and he left, never to be seen again. I then picked up the cash and walked down the hall to the office of the litigation partner and told him I had won the card cheating case and the client wanted to give the firm a bonus. I threw the stack of twenty-dollar bills on the desk. The partner carefully counted the money. "How did you get him off?" he asked.

"Oh, I just kept my cool," I said, "and did a lot of listening and let the big boys do all the work. The prosecutor made a deal with the others but not me, so when I said I was ready to go to trial, he dropped the charges because it wasn't worth the expense of a trial for only one of the accused."

The partner smiled and I think my stock in the firm went up that day—but not quite far enough.

WITHIN A FEW years, I was out-billing many of the partners, but you had to be an associate for ten years before the firm would consider you for partnership. I was not prepared to wait ten years, and they were not prepared to bend the rules—at least not for an ambitious newcomer like me. At the age of thirty, I was on an interchange track.

I decided, on a bit of a whim, to apply to the MBA program at Harvard and sent off a lengthy application a few days before the deadline. I missed any chance of early acceptance, but I did get an interview and flew to Boston to meet with the admissions dean.

"We don't train business owners; we train business managers," he said. "You fit the profile of an entrepreneur. Most of our graduates are management types. They want to manage big companies but are unlikely to start them."

It was a long interview and I was surprised at the amount of time he had spent analyzing my application and, by extension, me. Despite my entrepreneurial profile, I was short-listed for the MBA program, and once a week for the next several months, a letter would arrive in the mail with the Harvard crest on it telling me where I stood on the admissions list. Soon my life began to revolve around The List and I did not like the feeling. I was letting outside forces determine my future, which, for me, was paralyzing. I called the admissions dean.

"Take me off the list," I said.

As much as I wanted a Harvard education, I wanted my independence more. Ironically, I would make it to Harvard three times in my life—twice in my sixties and once in my seventies—but under very different circumstances. Knowing that as a younger man would not have changed my decision. It would have validated it.

I had lived all my life in Alberta and most of it in Edmonton, but I was afraid that if I did not leave the Edmonton law firm, I would become entrenched and never leave. It was not the life I wanted, so I decided to quit and move to Vancouver, a city I loved. I also decided that the great clientele I had worked so hard to acquire deserved a lawyer I liked and respected, so before I left, I referred them to the classmate who had turned down Firm A for Firm B. He appreciated the gesture and remains a close friend to this day.

I left Edmonton on November 15, 1968, in a 1969 Mercury Cougar convertible. It was the first new car I had ever owned and came fully loaded with everything an unemployed thirty-year-old lawyer could want. I had ordered it earlier that fall from an Edmonton Mercury dealer who proudly displayed a large billboard advertising the car on the roof of the dealership. "At the Sign of the Cat!" it said and featured an attractive young woman holding onto the leash of a big cat. The car came in a variety of colours. I went with yellow.

Leaving Edmonton was easy in many ways because there was no family home to sell and no round of family goodbyes to make. My mother had died suddenly in 1964, my sisters were busy with their own lives, and my father had sold the house and moved to the coast, where he would meet and marry an attractive widow named Ruby Stone. There had been a round of farewell dinners for me the week before, but my apartment had been rented and the contents were now in a moving van on their way to Vancouver. It was time to pack up the Cougar and go. I remember that it was a fairly typical Edmonton day weather-wise—about ten degrees below zero—but I decided to keep the top down until I got to the edge of town. It was a long drive to Vancouver and when I got to the railroad town of Valemount, I passed the turnoff to Canoe River and kept driving.

When I quit the Edmonton law firm, I never looked back and I never had a moment of regret. It was clear to me then that if I was not cut out to work in someone else's law firm, I would have to start my own. It was the second-best decision of my life and marked in many ways the break between my early years and the years that lay ahead. The foundation in place, it was time for me to get on with a life of my own making.

A Family Business

7

Partnership

A GOOD BUSINESS opportunity can make a man lose perspective. It was 1972, and after a long and somewhat convoluted courtship, Brenda and I were getting married. We had been living together for about eighteen months, but one morning in April, I came to my senses and asked her to marry me. She said yes. I said when. She said why.

I said, "Well, I have a business meeting in New York next Monday, so how about we get married on Saturday and then go to New York."

"For the meeting," she said.

"And the honeymoon," I said.

"Who else is coming, David?" she said.

"Fred Stimpson and Nelson Skalbania," I said, "but just for the meeting."

NOW IN TRUTH, I did not arrive in Vancouver in 1968 entirely broke, although I was certainly unemployed. I would have to wait until I was called to the bar in January before I could get back to work as a lawyer, but in the meantime, I was flush with a bit of capital earned from my first real business deal.

After my mother died, my father decided to sell the house and move to Vancouver. He was retired and wanted a break from the Edmonton winters. I knew he was restless and had no argument with him about the joys of shovelling snow, but I did have a few ideas for his exit strategy.

Dad had a good pension from CN, but between the value of his pension and the value of his house, he did not have enough money to purchase a house in the Vancouver market. So I asked him to sell me his Edmonton house but postpone payment for twelve months, during which I would put together the financing to replace the house with an apartment building. Dad agreed with my plan and moved to the coast, where he rented a small apartment. A year later and on schedule, I sold the Edmonton apartment building for a nice profit and paid him in full, with a little extra, to get him into the B.C. housing market.

Encouraged by my success, I then financed and built some apartments and a motor hotel in Jasper, Alberta, in partnership with Frank McDaniel, who was a legal client of mine. Those projects went well, so when I made the decision to move to Vancouver, Frank bought me out.

So when I arrived in Vancouver, I wasn't just another guy in a yellow convertible. I had a little start-up capital. I was cautious, though, and decided to open offices in the outlying municipality of Richmond rather than Vancouver to keep my overhead down. I worked in my little Richmond firm sixteen hours a day and soon had a booming real estate finance practice with several paralegals on staff. After five months, I was able to move my practice downtown to the Bentall Centre. It was one of the best buildings in Vancouver and the perfect location for an ambitious lawyer with a passion for real estate. I remember standing at the window of my new office, surrounded by boxes and legal files. What a view! And then, head down, I went back to work.

Within a few years, I was making more money than seemed possible for a guy who almost failed contracts law, but I was killing myself and knew I couldn't keep it up. I recruited George Hungerford and Richard Simon, and the firm of McLean, Hungerford & Simon was born. We specialized in real estate, corporate law, and finance, and in the booming economic times of the 1970s, we were very financially successful. But as time passed, I found myself increasingly involved in my own real estate deals. It was law by day and business by night, and it was exhausting. I needed perspective, and like all driven people, my lens on what was important in this world was narrowing to the size of a dollar sign.

FLASHBACK | EDMONTON 1968

Enter Brenda Mary Catherine McCuaig.

We met in an elevator. She was stunning, and I was mesmerized.

"And who might you be?" I said with what I hoped was sufficient charm to make a lasting impression. She took pity on me and laughed. It was a terrible opening line.

She was, I learned later, the great-granddaughter of Alexander Cameron Rutherford, the first premier of Alberta and co-founder of the University of Alberta. The law library at the U of A was housed in the Rutherford Library, and I must have passed under the portrait of Alexander Rutherford a dozen times a week as a student, but the girl in the elevator did not look a bit like him. He was portly. She was not. He had a handlebar moustache. Not Brenda. He had a receding hairline. She had beautiful hair. He wore old-fashioned spectacles. The girl in the elevator had clear blue eyes. No glasses.

It was as if God had finally sent me the life partner I had always wanted. I knew it instantly, but there were obstacles. We had a few daytime dates, but I was getting ready to move to Vancouver and Brenda had another suitor. You would think our story would have ended there, but it did not. I believe if something is meant to happen and both parties are open in their hearts, it will. I have evidence.

I moved to Vancouver in 1968 and Brenda married her other suitor in the spring and moved to Los Angeles. I met a young singer who lived in Toronto and spent my week-ends commuting back and forth between Vancouver and Toronto. It was not an ideal situation for either of us.

FLASH FORWARD | VANCOUVER 1970

The universe finally got its act together on a Sunday evening in September. I had just arrived home from the airport and the phone was ringing.

"It's Brenda," she said.

"Where are you?"

"I'm at the airport," she said.

"Stay right where you are. I'm on my way. Look for the yellow convertible."

She had a wonderful laugh.

Brenda joined me in 1970 and we were married eighteen months later. Like me, she had a passion for real estate and quickly became an insightful advisor. Unlike me, she saw beneath the surface of things. She also knew when to take a breath and slow down.

With Brenda's input and advice, my first B.C. project was a Burnaby apartment building I purchased with Graham Downey who had been a partner in the Edmonton apartment building built on my father's land. The Burnaby building consisted of twenty rental suites, but they were slow to rent. The new B.C. Condominium Act had just been passed, so I studied the act and decided to convert the building to condominiums. I then offered to buy out Graham Downey, and he agreed, so a few months later, I owned the building, which was now the second bona fide condominium in the province. This made me something of a pioneer and it wasn't long before my legal practice became the leading firm in condominium law in B.C. This led to an invitation to lecture to the Mortgage Brokers Association on condominium law, which led to more clients. In the meantime, Brenda and I spent our weekends driving out to Burnaby to flog condominiums. They still weren't selling, so Brenda suggested we redo the floors.

"They're beautiful hardwood floors," I said, "why change them?"

"Because most of the people we're seeing are young families and they won't have a lot of furniture yet," she said. "Children play on the floor, David, so let's give them wall-to-wall carpeting."

It worked like a charm. In a few months, all of the units were sold and we made $100,000 net after expenses, which was a handsome sum in 1970. I now had the capital I needed for my next project—the purchase of the old Eaton's store in Vancouver.

This was a much bigger venture and I needed experienced partners, so I decided to approach Nelson Skalbania, whom I had met playing basketball at the YMCA. Nelson and Fred Stimpson, another Vancouver developer, agreed to come in with me and we each put up one-third of $200,000 and made an offer. After some negotiating, we bought the old Eaton's store at the corner of Hastings and Seymour for $2.2 million, payable at $200,000 down and the balance in two years when Eaton's moved to their new store, without interest. That was a very good deal!

We then had to figure out what to do with it, so we hired an architect and drew up plans for a fifty-storey office tower. It was a grand scheme, but we needed to finance it. I had met Michael Spohn, an Eaton's executive, when we bought the Eaton's store, and he had introduced me to Disque D. Deane, a prominent New York developer and financier who had just launched a major real estate fund, Corporate Property Investors. Disque Deane was also a senior partner at Lazard Frères & Co., chairman of the Deane Group, and a partner (with Andre Meyer) in the later development and financing of Starrett City in Brooklyn. I felt like a mouse tackling an elephant—but nothing ventured, nothing gained.

To obtain financing from someone like Disque Deane, I knew we would need a high-profile tenant, so I contacted Sears, who were planning an expansion into British Columbia. We built a beautiful model of a new Sears store and then flew to Toronto to present it in person to the Sears executives. The model was not ready until the day before our meeting, though, so we booked a night flight—a pattern that would repeat itself a few months later when we went to New York.

Nelson and I arrived in Toronto and loaded the model onto a rental truck. We had not slept much but arrived with five minutes to spare and walked into a boardroom filled with three-button-suit Toronto executives. Undaunted, we set up the model and proceeded to make our pitch. Nelson spoke about the design and I talked about what a great opportunity it would be for Sears to move into the old Eaton's store, which had an established retail location and other attributes and so on and so forth. We spoke enthusiastically for about three-quarters of an hour and then stopped.

"Are there any questions?" I said.

There was a long pause and the chairman of Sears, an older gentleman who looked very dapper in his Toronto attire, looked at us over his glasses. "You guys ought to be in show business!" he said.

And with that, the meeting was over. We were ushered out and told they would "get back to us," which sounded like the hook, but a few days later, we got a call from a VP in their real estate division who said they were very interested. Negotiations ensued, and after several months, we signed a deal.

Next stop—New York City.

I worked feverishly on the financial package for several weeks and, when it was ready, called Disque Deane, who agreed to meet with us in New York but only if his office could review the package ahead of time. No problem. We sent it off and got a call back from Deane's office a few days later agreeing to meet with us the following Monday.

I RETURN NOW to my wedding day and the importance of not letting a good business opportunity skew a man's perspective. Brenda and I got married on a Saturday and left from Seattle on Sunday night, accompanied by Nelson Skalbania and Fred Stimpson. The plan was to fly all night and arrive in New York on Monday morning at seven o'clock. This would give us three hours to get to our hotel, freshen up, rehearse the pitch, and make the meeting.

I had never taken a sleeping pill but, for some reason, decided to take one that night so that I would get some sleep and be sharp for the meeting. Unfortunately, I took it two hours into a five-hour flight and by the time we reached New York, I was out like a light. My travelling companions helped me stagger off the plane, but I fell into a deep sleep in the cab on the way to the hotel. It was now eight o'clock, two hours before the meeting, and I was sleeping like a baby. And since I was the only one who had actually met Disque Deane, my attendance at the meeting was essential. For this, however, I would have to be conscious.

Brenda dragged me up to our hotel room and, with assistance from Fred and Nelson, got me undressed and into the shower where I began to wake up fast. I knew I was disoriented but not so far gone I wasn't socially alarmed by the circumstances. They then plied me with coffee, dragged me back downstairs (fully dressed, I hasten to add), and hauled me off to the meeting. We rehearsed our pitch in

the cab and arrived on time and ready. It was, as they say, show time.

In a nutshell, our proposal was that the New York fund would put up all of the money to buy the land, pay us $15,000 per month in management fees for the next year, and we would be equal partners. We would finish all the working drawings, get the permits needed from the city, finalize the Sears lease, and be ready to start construction. They would fund all the development costs during this period and arrange the construction financing when we started construction.

Disque Deane was a typical hyperactive New York businessman, and when we arrived for the meeting, we were told he was on the telephone.

"Take a seat," his assistant said. "He'll be right with you."

We waited about an hour and then Disque came out of his office holding a telephone. We all stood up.

"Take a seat," he said. "I'll be right with you."

We all sat down, waited another hour, and sometime around noon, he came out of his office a second time and invited us in. We got up, went in, sat down, and prepared to make the pitch, but the conversation was fairly one-sided and went something like this: "We've reviewed your deal and we like it and the terms are fine so we have a deal and you'll get a letter in a couple of days."

We were astonished—it was all of our Christmases at once! The meeting was over and it was back to the hotel for a celebratory lunch, goodbye to Fred and Nelson, and hello to my honeymoon.

Brenda and I had been married in a very simple ceremony with a few close friends in attendance, and I can't remember if we said "I do" or "I will," but we said something affirmative and signed the contract. I remember, though, that I was tremendously relieved and happy to be married to Brenda and wanted to celebrate the first week of our marriage in style.

We spent a couple of nights in New York and then, on a whim, flew to Atlanta. We both wanted to see the city and had heard about a glass elevator at the new Hyatt Regency hotel. It was one of the first of its kind in North America and the talk of the construction industry. One evening, as we waited in line to take the elevator up to the revolving restaurant at the top of the hotel, we struck up a conversation with the couple next to us.

Anne and Bill Stembler were Atlanta born, which meant they were charming, warm-hearted, and gracious. By the time we got to the top of the hotel, they had invited us to join them for a drink and dinner. And by the time dinner was over, they had invited us to a very old Atlanta club for the annual debutante ball later that week. We accepted the invitation and enjoyed a night right out of *Gone with the Wind*. It was the start of a very special bond and a reminder to me that business relationships were not enough. I needed friends and I needed love and I needed to be around people who brought out the best in me. For some reason, I kept meeting those people in elevators.

After a wonderful week in Atlanta, we arrived back in Vancouver refreshed. Brenda went back to her job at the Vancouver Art Gallery, and I turned my attention to the next phase of the Eaton's store project, which we had decided to call Vancouver Square. It was detailed work, but we got the permits and working drawings completed on time, and true to his word, Disque Deane funded it all, advancing us a sum in excess of $1 million.

Midway through the process he decided to visit Vancouver. It was his first trip to Vancouver and he loved the city. "Tremendous potential," he kept saying, which was music to our Canadian ears.

A few months later, he called singing a different tune. Tremendous potential notwithstanding, he had decided Vancouver was too far away from New York for his office to supervise the deal. They were prepared to let us out of the deal with nothing for their equity, though, if we paid back the money they had already advanced.

And with that, all of our Christmases were cancelled.

We had just completed all of the drawings and were ready to go to bid, and we had no more financing. We decided to put the project out to bid anyway, but inflation was rampant in the mid-1970s and prices came in well over our budget. We cut anything from the drawings we could without jeopardizing the project, but again, the bids came in way over our budget.

I called Nelson and Fred and said we had to find another partner fast, and after a series of meetings with potential investors, we settled on Lord Realty, a firm owned by a wealthy family in Hamburg looking for investments in Canada. We also hired Morley Koffman, a well-known corporate and real estate lawyer. With Morley on board, we began negotiations with Lord Realty, but unlike the speed of the deal we did with Disque Deane, this one would be slow and laborious.

Our goal was to negotiate a joint venture in which Lord Realty would be the money and we would be the developer and manager, but we knew if there was a hiccup of any kind (as there invariably is in such deals), they would blow us away without a second thought.

I met with Nelson and Fred again and suggested we get another party involved. There were a lot of investors looking for deals in Vancouver, and I strongly suspected that if we could line up another offer, Lord Realty would match or better it.

"They've spent a lot of time on this," I said, "and their egos are so big, they won't want to lose it now."

Nelson went to work and produced two more parties who expressed interest in the project. Armed with this information, we went to the next meeting with Lord Realty and said we didn't think a joint venture would work after all and had interest from two other buyers who wanted to purchase the project from us.

That got their attention and after a relatively short negotiation, we made a deal to sell Vancouver Square to Lord Realty for all of the funds Disque Deane had advanced plus interest and $1.5 million for us. The deal closed quickly and I took my third. Inflation continued to roar and I was very glad we got out of the deal when we did. As for Vancouver Square, Lord Realty dramatically changed the concept, built the project, and retain ownership of it today some forty years later.

MY NEXT DEAL would take me to the Supreme Court of Canada.

I'd heard that Eaton's needed a new warehouse in Edmonton and were prepared to sell their downtown warehouse to whoever built the new one. Since I knew the city so well, I flew to Edmonton to check things out and found a large building site in the northeast corner of the city.

Once again, I invited Nelson and Fred to participate in the deal, knowing we all had some capital. Nelson had an engineering firm and was associated with an architectural firm, so we agreed that they would handle the design. We bought Eaton's downtown property (a full city block) for $2.4 million. We put $400,000 down with the balance due when they moved into the new warehouse. Eaton's liked us and these were good terms.

We decided not to go with the land in northeast Edmonton and, instead, optioned land for the new warehouse from the City of Edmonton. The City wanted to attract industrial tenants, so they were offering a 20 percent discount on the value of the land if we agreed to build on it within three years. We readily agreed, signed the deal, and got to work. This incurred the wrath of the individual who owned the land in northeast Edmonton, who proceeded to sue us as a taxpayer in the City of Edmonton, alleging the City had favoured us with a 20 percent discount. We won at trial and on appeal, but the plaintiff then appealed to the Supreme Court of Canada. I had never been to the Supreme Court in Ottawa as a lawyer and would now be going as a party to a lawsuit.

We hired Louis Desrochers, QC, and when the judges came in and the hearing started, they gave the appellant and his lawyer a tough time. To paraphrase, it was something along the lines of: "You are alleging that your client is coming to court claiming he is grieved as a City of Edmonton taxpayer. We have read the file and the truth is he is trying to get the deal set aside so he can sell the defendants his land. He is not in court with clean hands."

Clean hands! The court had spoken. In a matter of minutes, they dismissed the application for leave to appeal and the lawsuit was over. We could now proceed.

Construction started early in 1974 and was completed in the fall. It was never our intention to be long-term investors and we had made arrangements to sell the new warehouse to a pension fund. We were ready to close the sale when I got the sense that the pension fund was getting cold feet. Inflation was high and the spokespeople for the pension fund were as nervous as the rest of us. To protect themselves, they raised the issue of a warranty on the roof in case of a leak.

"We will not only warranty it," I said, "we will guarantee the two-year warranty with a letter of credit sufficient to rebuild the roof."

The "sufficient credit" amounted to $150,000, so they agreed and we closed with a great sigh of relief. Two years later, the warranty expired and we got our letter of credit back.

In the meantime, Nelson was jumpy to sell the downtown warehouse and city block we had bought from Eaton's, but I had been very careful when we structured that deal to have a provision in it that if either or both of Nelson and/or Fred wanted to sell, I would have the first right of refusal to buy. It was a provision that was about to teach me everything I needed to know about partnerships.

ON AUGUST 9, 1973, Brenda gave birth to our first child, Jason David Duncan McLean. I was a very happy father—grateful beyond all measure to my wife and emotionally overwhelmed by the generosity of the universe. Thanks to Brenda, and to his own good nature, Jason was an easy baby, so when he was just three weeks old, we decided to take a family trip. Our plan was to fly to Montreal, rent a car, and then drive down the east coast through New England. From there, we would head south to Atlanta to visit our friends Anne and Bill Stembler.

We were just about to leave when I got a phone call from Nelson telling me he had a deal to sell the Eaton's downtown land for $2.7 million.

"It's a $300,000 profit," he said. "We should take it."

"I don't agree," I said, "and I have first right of refusal, so I'll buy you and Fred out."

I hung up and immediately signed two cheques for $25,000, one for each of them. They were deposits on the purchase according to the terms of our agreement with a closing in sixty days. Brenda and I then left on our trip, but when we returned, the cheques were back on my desk with a letter from my partners refusing to sell to me. They were having second thoughts, and I couldn't blame them for that, because a year later, we did end up selling to Nelson's buyer, but for $4.4 million instead of $2.7 million, which net us a profit of $2 million. My share was $675,000 instead of $2 million, but *c'est la vie*. You live—so you might as well learn from the experience.

WHEN BRENDA AND I were married, I told her I did not want my secretary to know more about my business activities than my wife. I was an entrepreneur to my core, so there would be risks, challenges, and, I hoped, a few rewards along the way, but at no point would there be deception. I had seen too many entrepreneurs whose families knew virtually nothing about their business lives and the chaos that ensued when the business or the entrepreneur failed.

But in Brenda, I knew I had found the perfect partner in life and in business. And with that certainty, the McLean Group was born. I now had a family and a family business. I had a partner I could trust with my life and, in 1973, a son who looked like executive material with or without a soother in his mouth. The McLean Group would begin as a real estate investment and development firm with me as chairman and CEO and Brenda as vice-chair. In the blink of an eye—about forty years to be precise—it would transition into a second-generation family business active in real estate, film and television production, telecommunications, and aviation. Our family would grow with the arrival of our second son, Sacha Rutherford Franklin McLean, in 1975, and by 1985, I would leave the practice of law and run my family business full time.

In the meantime, there were apartments to buy, land to develop, heritage buildings to restore, interest rates to contend with, and bankers to tame. I would learn some important lessons about leadership in each of these areas.

8

"If you aren't in over your
head, how do you know
how tall you are?"

T.S. ELIOT

Growth

IN THE MID-1970S, I turned my attention to the United States.
Brenda was busy on the home front, so I went to California
and bought three hundred apartment units in Sacramento.
It was a bargain, price-wise, but 30 percent of the apartments were vacant. I scratched my head after a tour of the
property, trying to figure out a solution to the high vacancy
rates. I then tried something no one else had done. I raised
the rent. It seemed the previous owners had underesti-
mated the market and because the rents were so low, prospective tenants thought there must be something wrong
with the building. Within four months, the vacancy was
reduced to less than 5 percent and the property was gener-
ating cash flow.

I had an outside equity investor on this project who
wanted a quick return on his money, so after a few renovations, we put the building back on the market. It sold

within two months for an outstanding profit. In those days, a capital gain in the U.S. was tax-free to a Canadian company or partnership under a tax treaty between Canada and the U.S. It was taxed in Canada, but we had losses, so we sheltered all the gain.

Encouraged by this experience, we then bought and sold apartments in Santa Rosa, California; Atlanta, Georgia; and Hawaii. Once again, we sheltered the gains and ended up with some equity capital that we brought back to Canada. We used a portion of the capital to buy two high-rise apartment buildings in Ottawa from an insurance company. They were anxious to sell, so we negotiated excellent terms. Ontario had rent controls in place, but we were able to raise rents 6 percent a year and pass capital improvements on to the tenants.

We sold both buildings at a profit a year later, but I was beginning to feel we should invest closer to home and Brenda was in agreement. We shared an interest in heritage buildings and decided to look for opportunities in that area of the market.

BRENDA HAD WORKED as an art curator and had a good eye for historical detail. She also had a family background that fostered an appreciation for protecting heritage buildings. Her great-grandfather Alexander Rutherford had built Edmonton's Rutherford House in 1911, and his family had lived in it until 1940. Brenda's father, Eric McCuaig, was born there. It was a grand house on a large lot near the University of Alberta campus overlooking the North Saskatchewan River. Rutherford sold it to the university he had co-founded after his wife, Mattie Birkett, died in 1940, and the Delta Upsilon fraternity occupied it until 1968.

Fraternity boys are not dream tenants for a heritage home badly in need of restoration, and by 1966, the house had deteriorated so much it was slated for demolition. A campaign was launched by the Alberta Women's Club to restore and protect the house as a historic site. They were successful and today Rutherford House is open to the public and contains family items donated by Brenda's grandmother Hazel Rutherford McCuaig, who grew up in the house.

With history in mind, our first heritage purchase was a building in the Gastown area of Vancouver known as Hudson House. It was the original Hudson's Bay warehouse, built in 1895, and had been damaged in a fire, but we loved the building and saw past the problems. Over the next two years, we renovated it and it quickly filled with tenants who shared our appreciation for heritage real estate. In the process, we learned there was a vast difference between restoration and renovation and that our skills lay firmly in the latter area.

Restoration projects are generally financed by government bodies or foundations committed to restoring a public building to its former grandeur exactly as it was originally designed. Such projects are more concerned with historical accuracy than commercial viability. As renovators, we were looking for buildings with historical charm that could lend themselves to changing or upgrading the function of the building for a more modern purpose. We quickly learned that not every older building should be renovated and that the decision to do so was largely determined by the building's cost, quality, location, potential for future use, and structural uniqueness. Many of the older buildings we looked at did not have sufficient floor space to justify the expense of renovation. Warehouse buildings, however, were built with more floor space, which gave us an excellent use of interior space without the necessity of rebuilding external structures.

In addition to Hudson House, which we owned until the late 1990s, I had my eye on another heritage property in Gastown. This one consisted of a block of three buildings on Water Street just east of the old Canadian Pacific Railway station (today known as Waterfront Station). After a little detective work, I found out who the owner was and flew to New York for a meeting. The properties were owned by a large public company that had lost interest in them, so they agreed to sell. Collectively, the three buildings were a big property with more than 400,000 square feet of space, but I used some of my profits from other deals to buy it with financing from a bank for 75 percent of the price. A year later, I sold off the two buildings on the eastern end of the block and with the proceeds paid off the financing on the balance of the block, which consisted of a seven-storey building of approximately 250,000 square feet called The Landing.

It was a beautiful Edwardian-style warehouse on the Vancouver waterfront built in 1905, originally known as the Kelly Douglas Building. We bought it in 1972 and immediately began preparations for its renovation. It would take us several years and the partnership of others, but in the end, we would be well rewarded personally and financially for the cost and effort of getting it right. The renovation of 375 Water Street was a labour of love.

In the meantime, we focussed on upgrading the cash flow from existing tenants. The Landing, at the time, was home to a number of businesses engaged in the manufacture of clothing, and many of their employees were from China and Hong Kong. I suspect that some of them lacked work visas, because whenever we dropped by for a visit, heads would disappear under work stations only to reappear when we left. They may have thought we were from the immigration department, but I can't say for sure. Their employers, however, were about to pay a little more rent, because the existing rents at the time of our purchase were around forty cents net per square foot, which was insufficient to cover our costs. It took a few years, but we gradually increased rents to a more appropriate $4 per square foot, which positioned the value of the building for renovation.

We did some preliminary designs and cost out the price of a complete renovation, which would include upgrading the building to current earthquake standards. It looked like we would need $20 million, not including the cost of the land, to make it work. I realized this was too big a deal to go it alone and we would need an equity partner, so I approached my friend Ken Wall, who worked for North American Life. Ken told me that the Canadian Pacific pension fund was looking for real estate investments in Vancouver and arranged for me to meet with the pension fund's president, Gerry Cloutier.

I am forever grateful he did, because Gerry was a wonderful man. He was an astute businessman with a big heart. In time, we became good friends, and he was a guardian angel to me when interest rates shot through the roof in 1986 and I was struggling to stay afloat. But all of that lay ahead, and in 1982, we sold 50 percent of The Landing to the Canadian Pacific pension fund for $4.5 million. Our cost for this half interest was less than $500,000, so we had a big capital gain. As part of the deal, we agreed to obtain construction financing and proceed with the renovation.

Work began in the spring of 1983 with completion forecast for 1985. We had learned a lot about construction from our experience renovating Hudson House and were able to convince our structural engineers to design the building so that the windows could be preserved without steel bracing. I was familiar with the value of using a transfer beam to stabilize a building during an earthquake, but in the case of our building, it came with additional advantages. By placing two huge reinforced concrete staircases at each end of the building, we were able to put in a large reinforced concrete transfer beam on the second floor. This enabled us to preserve the views from all of the windows.

As construction proceeded, we had to contend with a construction strike and escalating interest rates. The former was inconvenient, but the latter was a nightmare. By the start of 1985, the prime rate was well over 15 percent, and since most of our financing was based on prime, we were getting badly hurt by high interest rates. I had never experienced such tough economic conditions in my life, and I hope not to repeat the experience.

To complicate matters, we had investments in San Francisco and Hawaii that badly needed cash and we were rapidly running out of liquidity.

The Hudson House project had given us experience renovating a small heritage office building with retail on the ground floor. The apartment buildings in Sacramento had given us experience in California. I decided to combine these two experiences and look for a project similar in size and scope to Hudson House in San Francisco's downtown waterfront area. It was a city that fascinated me, and when the Reagan government passed a tax law designed to encourage urban renewal in major American cities, I was intrigued. The law allowed a substantial depreciation rate for the renovation of commercial buildings over a certain age. To my entrepreneurial brain, that sounded like an opportunity.

I contacted a San Francisco appraiser named Joe Parker, who had done some previous work for us on California apartment appraisals for banking financing. Joe was an old-school guy with good values. I flew to San Francisco to meet him for lunch in the hope of getting a reference to a good office broker. He referred me to his nephew Jeff Congdon, who worked for Cushman & Wakefield, a large brokerage company with offices in San Francisco.

Jeff was well acquainted with the market, and we began looking at properties. After a brief search, I decided to make an offer on an eighty-thousand-square-foot warehouse building near the Embarcadero that could be converted to offices and retail. It was on Steuart Street, so I named the project Steuart Place. (The unusual spelling is said to be left over from an eighteenth-century version of the name.)

We put together an investment package covering all of the renovating costs plus the cost of the building itself and began to look for an investor who could use the depreciation. Jeff recommended the Twigg-Smith family in Honolulu, who owned a lot of property there, including its major newspaper, the *Honolulu Advertiser*.

The Twigg-Smiths were a talented and interesting family with deep roots in Hawaii's history. They were the descendants of two of Hawaii's first missionary families. Thurston Twigg-Smith was a Yale-educated engineer and the recipient of a Bronze Star for five European campaigns as a captain in the field artillery during World War II. In addition to running the family business, he was a well-known philanthropist and art patron. I very much wanted to meet him. There is an old expression in Hawaii that the missionaries from New England came to Hawaii to do good and stayed and did well. The Twigg-Smiths were living proof of that expression in both areas.

We sent them some preliminary information and they agreed to meet with us in San Francisco. They liked us and they liked the project, so were able to move quickly and structure a deal in which they would provide 80 percent of the equity for the first two years and then split the equity with us fifty-fifty. This enabled us to invest only 20 percent of the up front equity. As part of the deal, we would also manage the project, do all the renovations (for which we would be paid a management fee), and have Jeff Congdon handle the leasing.

The project went well from the start and within two years we had it almost fully leased, including a commitment from Vancouver's legendary restaurateur Umberto Menghi to put in a restaurant on the lower floor. Umberto was a good friend and we partnered with him on a restaurant at our Hudson House building in Vancouver called Al Porto.

Everything was running smoothly until San Francisco had an earthquake. Fortunately, our building had been upgraded to the current earthquake standards and came through quite well, but many tenants were very nervous, as were our bankers. Nervous bankers made me nervous, and as our construction financing was due to be repaid in six months, I talked to the Twigg-Smiths about arranging permanent financing with a Canadian bank.

It was 1983 and I had just become chairman of the board of governors at the University of British Columbia and among the other board members was a director of Scotiabank. He was familiar with my real estate investment business and had approached me on an earlier occasion to ask if I would like to do some business with Scotiabank. I called him and told him about the San Francisco project and he liked the idea, as they had just opened an office in San Francisco. He also liked the idea of developing a relationship with the Twigg-Smiths.

I met with the bank's loan officers in San Francisco and they were very receptive, so we put the application together, which they sent to the credit people in Toronto. On a side note, our construction lender was the Mercantile Bank of Canada, a small bank specializing in construction loans that was owned by Citibank in New York. The Mercantile Bank was the type of lender that raised money on the open market at low interest rates and then turned around and loaned money to borrowers for a small interest rate spread. As interest rates escalated, the bank came under intense pressure, as most of their loans were now underwater, so the much higher rates on the open market were a serious liability. They were understandably anxious, then, to have our loan repaid.

I was also on the board of Nu-West Development Corporation in Calgary, which was one of the largest landowners and housing developers in North America. The escalating interest rates were making them jittery, like everyone else, and had become a major topic of discussion at board meetings. I was in Calgary for one of those meetings when I got a call from Scotiabank's San Francisco loan manager.

Our loan had been turned down.

"Declined?" I said.

"Yes."

"Why?"

It had gone to the credit department in Toronto, I was told, but Peter Godsoe, chairman of the credit committee (and later, CEO of Scotiabank) said they did not want to take over "a bad Mercantile Bank loan."

A bad loan? I was astounded, as the loan was in good standing and we had never missed a payment.

"Stay by your phone," I said to the unfortunate messenger from San Francisco. "This is not a final decision!"

I immediately phoned my colleague on the UBC board of governors who had approached me on behalf of the bank in the first place. He was furious and said he would make some calls. I heard later that he called the CEO, Cedric Ritchie. He had spoken to Cedric before the loan went to credit and at the time Cedric had said he would support it.

"I told them to red tag that file and if there was a problem to call me," Cedric said to my UBC colleague.

Within an hour, Cedric had asked for the file and spoken with Peter Godsoe, and the loan was approved. The banker from San Francisco called me with the news. She was incredulous.

"I've never seen a loan get turned around so fast," she said.

I knew Cedric Ritchie in 1983 only by reputation, but twelve years later, I got to know him well when he was appointed to the CN board. He was on the board during the year of the IPO and for many years thereafter, and when he retired, he was named a director emeritus for his outstanding service to CN. Cedric was CEO of Scotiabank for twenty-five years because he was a great person and a great CEO. Years later, when I got to know him a bit better, I mentioned the loan. He remembered it well and said in his straightforward way, "I approved it because it was good for the bank."

With the loan in place, we agreed to sell our interest in Steuart Place to our Hawaiian partners, the Twigg-Smiths. We had done well on the investment and because they had taken so much depreciation on the building, they wanted to own it completely to avoid any tax recapture. Our partnership with the Twigg-Smiths had been a good one and we would often visit them on trips to Hawaii.

But we were not out of the woods yet.

CHRISTMAS 1985
It was a few days before Christmas and I was in Toronto, desperately trying to arrange financing on some of our other projects. It was not going well. The high interest rates had wreaked havoc with the loan market. Banks were looking for big spreads and they wanted guarantees on

everything. I had a sleepless night, and in the morning, I took the first flight home.

Brenda was always my best advisor and I knew we needed to put an end to our financial stress. I told her I was going to devote the next full year of my life to solving the problems and stabilizing our business and our family. My plan was to approach our lead banker but I knew I would need a cash source to settle our corporate debts before I did. I would also need to approach our two other bankers, with whom we held smaller loans, and get them all settled at once.

I called Gerry Cloutier and said I needed cash to get rid of our corporate loans and proposed to sell him 30 percent of The Landing plus two properties on Grandview Highway on the condition that we would have the right to buy them back within three years for the amount advanced plus interest at 6 percent.

He agreed—he was our guardian angel!

I called our lead banker the next day and spoke to the vice-president of credit, whom I knew quite well.

"I want you to put our company into special handling," I said, which is a banking term for companies that could no longer service their debt because of the huge interest rates.

"Why would you do that?" he said. "You're one of our best customers. You've never missed an interest payment."

"Not anymore," I said.

I told him I was tired of running around raising financing and selling property just to pay huge interest costs. It had to stop.

"So as of today," I said, "we will not be paying any more interest and want to find a way to settle our debt."

"Okay," he said, and within twenty-four hours our account was assigned to two workout specialists from the accounting side of the bank and the usual friendly faces we dealt with at the bank retreated from view. Welcome to special handling.

I hired Bernie Fahy, a retired accountant, who agreed to work with us to present a proposal to the bank. We also had one meeting with a group of lawyers who specialized in bankruptcy, which depressed me so much that I decided I would not (could not, will not) go that route. Instead, we sat down with the workout specialists and agreed on a framework that would lead to a proposal. They were, in fact, very fair and just wanted a realistic assessment of our assets and liabilities. It was now early March, but with Bernie Fahy's guidance, we prepared a binder showing all our assets and liabilities with a realistic valuation of what each asset could be sold for in the existing market by the end of April. We obtained letters of opinion on value from realtors who were highly respected in commercial real estate.

We presented the material to the bank at the end of April, and after a long meeting, they agreed to review it. Thank you very much, we said, but we were also planning to make them an offer to settle the debt for cash. They agreed to review our cash-for-debt proposal when it was ready, so it was back to the drawing board until the middle of May, when we presented an offer in writing to settle.

At the next meeting, the bankers said they had reviewed our binder of valuations and "in general" agreed with what we had presented. They had called a few other realtors to get confirmation of values and said our values were "in general" realistic. They said they would present it to the workout group at the bank in Toronto and get back to us. They had no comment on our cash-for-debt proposal. We waited four months and had no response, in general or otherwise, but that gave me time to close the deal I made with Gerry Cloutier, so we now had funds in a neutral bank.

Finally, at the end of September I received a call from the workout specialist, who said he had a response from credit but it was not what we proposed. My heart stopped.

"Instead of what you proposed, we need 5 percent more to cover our costs," he said.

I paused as long as I dared in an effort to keep myself from shouting hallelujah into the phone.

"Let me see what I can do," I said. "I'll call you in a day or so."

"Fine," he said.

I immediately went to the neutral bank to whom we owed nothing and where we had funds on deposit. I asked them for a $300,000 line of credit, and they agreed to give me $500,000 at prime plus 1 percent with no security except my signature. I then called the other banks and said we would agree to their terms on the condition that upon payment they would release all of our security and all of our guarantees.

They agreed.

On December 15, 1986, we closed with all three banks and I went home that night free of all bank debt except for the line of credit. All of our security was released. It had been almost a year to the day since my conversation with Brenda that I would get our financial house in order. A new kind of Christmas was coming, and I slept well for the first time in what felt like a very long time.

Timing in business is everything, and as we entered 1987, interest rates dropped dramatically with prime falling from 18 percent to 6 percent by the end of the year. Conversely, property values began to climb, so by the end of 1988, we were able to repay Gerry Cloutier with interest because of the sale of a couple of our non-core assets.

Nineteen eighty-six was a tough year but Brenda, as always, was solidly involved and very supportive. She may have entertained the thought of smothering me in my sleep from time to time, but she never acted on that thought. We decided that to apply the lessons we had learned, we needed to draft some guidelines for the future. We came up with ten:

1. Always be honest and straightforward with your bankers.
2. Always go to the bank with a solution not a problem.
3. Face tough times realistically and do not live on hope— take actions that will solve the problem not just postpone it.
4. Always keep your word once a promise is made.
5. Choose advisors who are realistic but will work through the problem. There are good people in the world who will help you if you ask and if you are very realistic.
6. Bankruptcy is never a good solution, so stay away from the bankruptcy lawyers—they are undertakers.
7. Don't be afraid to pray and ask for guidance—you will get help.
8. Listen to the vice-chair.
9. LISTEN to the vice-chair.
10. LISTEN TO THE VICE-CHAIR!

IT IS 1953 and I have just finished my first year of university. Most of my friends have jobs in the resort towns of Banff and Jasper, but I need to be home so I can save money and pay for my education. I get a job as a lifeguard at a public swimming pool in Edmonton. The job is great because it starts at one o'clock in the afternoon and finishes at nine at night, so I can get a job on the side selling advertising for the football program at the U of A. It is contract work, so the more I sell, the more I get paid! I follow up on contacts all over town, and at the end of the summer, I have money for my fees and expenses with enough left over to buy an old car.

I give my mother some spending money which we decide to call rent.

9

"A hunch is creativity trying
to tell you something."
FRANK CAPRA

Vancouver Film Studios

FOR MUCH OF MY business life, I saw value primarily in the hard assets of buildings, land, railroads, and other tangible commodities, but in the 1990s, I found myself drifting into the creative economy, which for my family business was the film and television industry.

Paintings I understood, and thanks to Brenda's eye, I had learned much about the value of art and became an avid collector. Music I loved, not as much as basketball, perhaps, but enough to really enjoy concerts. I admit I would rather hear a few good tenors belt out Leonard Cohen's "Hallelujah" than listen to an evening of chamber music, but for a boy who ditched his violin under a wooden sidewalk, I've come a long way.

The film industry was a different kind of creativity. Part circus and part military operation, film crews moved in convoys of trucks and gear. They set themselves up in old warehouses where they built enormous sets. They needed lumber and nails for those sets, mills for the carpenters, trailers for the actors, hotel rooms for the production executives, cars for the teamsters, parking for the cars, post-production services, art directors, camera crews, wardrobe designers, props, cranes, photocopiers, offices, lighting and grip equipment, walkie-talkies, cinematographers, helicopters for aerial shoots, and food! And the list goes on.

The McLean Group's move into this world was triggered by thirty-five acres of land in east Vancouver, a zoning problem, a health crisis, the boredom of Sacha McLean, and a eureka moment that took place in the middle of a Chrétien motorcade in Phoenix, Arizona.

I'll start with the real estate.

THE INTEREST CRISIS of the mid-1980s had led to the recapitalization of the McLean Group and the renewal of my entrepreneurial spirit. With economic conditions rapidly improving, The Landing officially opened on April 19, 1987. Our efforts to get it right had paid off and we were recognized by the City of Vancouver with accolades and awards for a heritage renovation that balanced the history of a beautiful old building with the health of a new one. Our partners in the project, Canadian Pacific Pension Investment Management, Soren Rasmussen (project architect), and James Pitcairn (construction manager), were a first-rate group, and Brenda and I shared a great sense of accomplishment in putting the team together.

During the renovation process, some good tenants had to move out, so to ease their disruption (and perhaps take advantage of it), I began looking around the city for a building to accommodate them. I settled on an area at the corner of Grandview Highway and Boundary Road that had a couple of small industrial buildings for sale. It was a good location about fifteen minutes from downtown and thirty minutes to the airport. Access to the Trans-Canada Highway was a few blocks east, which significantly added to its appeal as a long-term investment.

We made an offer on a building in the middle of the block between Boundary Road and Skeena Street, owned and occupied by Philips Electronics Canada. I liked the building and asked the manager why they were selling it. He said they needed more office space and less warehouse space. The wheels began to turn.

"I have a building under option on the corner of Boundary and Grandview Highway that has plenty of office space. Would you consider moving to that building on a lease?"

The manager knew the building and thought it might work, but he didn't have the authority to make the decision.

"Talk to head office," he said. "They're in Toronto."

Philips Electronics Canada is a division of Royal Philips Electronics, which is headquartered in the Netherlands and operates worldwide. I got the name of the president of Canadian operations, called him, and pitched a proposal to buy their building and move them two doors east.

"It has everything you need," I said. "And we can renovate to suit."

"I'm tight for time right now," he said, but agreed to consider the offer if I could prepare a proposal and come to Toronto on short notice.

"How about next Monday?" I said.

"Fine," he said.

It was Wednesday.

I met with our architect, Soren Rasmussen. He was working full time on The Landing, but we discussed a concept for Philips and within forty-eight hours Soren produced a layout design and a rough sketch. I loved it.

"Can you clean it up by Sunday?" I asked.

He could and he did, so I was off to Toronto on Sunday afternoon to meet with Philips the next day. The president looked over the plans, the rendering, and our lease proposal. He loved the location and the space.

"I can't believe you did this in three days," he kept saying.

As luck would have it, the chief financial officer, who was the grandson of the company's Dutch founder, was working in the Toronto office as part of his international training. He reviewed our proposal and liked our ideas, and within a few weeks the deal was done. Philips Canada moved into our building on the corner and their building was ours.

We now owned nearly five acres of buildings along Grandview Highway and I started to wonder if I could acquire the whole block. So when the building between the old Philips building and the one they were now leasing from us came up for sale, I bought it. We then looked at a huge building on the corner of Skeena and Grandview that was occupied by a Simmons Bedding Company. Unfortunately, it was controlled by a broker who decided to hold an auction. The building sold quickly, but the price, in my opinion, was too high. I had a funny feeling that sooner or later we would get it. We just needed to be patient.

The new owner decided to lease it to a start-up warehouse club from Toronto. A group of executives at a large food company had quit their jobs and joined forces to start a warehouse club of their own. Their plan was to raise $50 million of equity, which they did, and open warehouse clubs across Canada similar to Price Club and Costco. I watched from a distance and quietly acquired the last building on the block, which was owned by a tire company.

In the meantime, the Toronto warehouse boys came and went in their leased Jaguars demanding this, that, and the other thing from the new owner who agreed to put in all of the improvements they requested—to the tune of about $3 million. The new owner had paid $6 million for the land, so he was now into it for $9 million. The game plan changed abruptly when the warehouse club went into receivership a few months before it was scheduled to open. The tenants disappeared and the owner, who was one of the best housing developers in British Columbia, was left holding the bag.

He decided to sell the building. All that was left to do was pave the parking lot and put in the parking lights, and it would be finished. But a decision was made not to spend any more money on it, so the property sat vacant, waiting for buyers.

I was offered the property for $10 million and turned it down. It wasn't worth that much, and without a long-term tenant in place, it was far too risky. I had learned a few things in the 1980s. Several months went by and there were still no offers.

The owner's agents eventually came back to me, this time with the words I had been waiting for: "Make us an offer."

The owner was ready to sell and get back to doing what he did best—building houses.

"I'm going to make you an offer," I said, "but you won't like it."

I offered $6 million, which was what the owner had paid for the land a few years earlier. We made a deal and I closed within two months. Now all I needed was a tenant.

Word got out that I was the new owner of the building and I was approached by Edgar Kaiser, who also wanted to open a Canadian warehouse club. I had a meeting with his agent and outlined my lease terms: $1.2 million net annual rent and they would pay all operating costs plus a $1 million letter of credit securing the rent and operating costs on a ten-year lease.

We reached an agreement, providing I finished the parking lot and the lighting, which cost me $500,000. My all-in cost was $6.5 million. The warehouse club opened a few months later and two years later was bought by Price Club, who sold it to Costco, who stayed in that location for eighteen years. It was a great deal for everyone, and I never raised the rent. When Costco left, they were replaced by Walmart. This was something of a coup for the McLean Group, as it was the first Walmart in Vancouver.

I continued to acquire land in an adjoining block to the north that contained a variety of buildings, including a small industrial warehouse that had been converted into a sound stage called Northstar International Studios.

Vancouver producer Justis Greene and his partners had purchased it in 1985 and renovated it into what was considered at the time to be a sophisticated shooting and production space. By 1987, they were ready to get out of the landlord businesses and back into filmmaking, so they put their asset up for sale.

Well, we *were* in the landlord business, so we purchased Northstar with the intention of reconverting it back into a warehouse for long-term lease. In the meantime, it was in demand by local filmmakers who rarely stayed more than a few months. To my surprise, the return from film tenants in five to six months exceeded the rent I could get from a long-term tenant in a year.

It was clear that local filmmakers liked the facility and they especially liked its location, so as leases expired on our other warehouses in the area, our practice was to fill them with short-term film and television tenants until a more permanent tenant could be found. By the early 1990s, four of the fifteen buildings we owned were in semi-regular use by filmmakers. It provided short-term cash flow, which was helpful, but I had other plans for the area that did not involve film studios.

IT HAD TAKEN more than ten years, but by 1995, we had acquired thirty-five acres of property (approximately two city blocks) at the corner of Grandview Highway and Boundary Road. They were earning their keep, but my long-term plan was a commercial and residential development called Still Creek Village. I wanted to build something big. The concept was a planned community that blended employment opportunities with housing, open space, and community amenities. Uses would include industrial, wholesale, retail, residential, live/work amenities for employees and residents, and a diversity of public services.

The creek itself was one of only two remaining visible streams in urban Vancouver and the last evidence of what was once a watery network of streams threading the area. Most had been buried by culverts, roads, and industrial buildings, so restoring and enhancing the two surviving creeks had become a matter of public interest. Decades earlier, Still Creek had been almost completely destroyed when it was connected to a sewer and storm drain. We had committed to participating in the renewal of Still Creek in partnership with the City of Vancouver and a number of local environmental foundations.

Still Creek Village would protect our section of Still Creek and give the public better access to it. In addition to the primary land uses, our plan included support facilities such as restaurants, convenience retail, fitness centres, and daycares. Other amenities were park spaces on either side of the creek and designated areas for public art. We spent many months developing the project with the help of our talented design and architectural team. All we needed was approval of our rezoning application from the City—which we didn't get.

Now what? We were considering our options when a heart problem intervened. It was mine, of course.

SPRING 1996
All things considered, the timing was good, because our sons were not children or teenagers when a blocked artery

in my heart came close to ending my life. They were young men, and when Brenda and I needed them most, they were there for us. Sacha was in his last year of an honours degree in geography and economics at Queen's University in Kingston. Jason was closer to home in first-year law at the University of British Columbia. With their input, Brenda and I came up with a game plan that would keep the family business on course during my recovery. It many ways, this marked a transition in our roles and identities from a family business to a business family.

Jason and Sacha both offered to take a leave of absence from their studies, but Brenda and I felt that was unnecessary and unwise. We wanted them to stay on course and finish their degrees, and the McLean Group was not without leadership. We had, in fact, an excellent staff of committed employees who had earned our trust and respect. The real issue was my entrepreneurial need to be present.

In the end, the plan was simple. Sacha received permission from Queen's to finish his last semester at the University of British Columbia, Jason stayed in law school, I concentrated on my recovery, and Brenda, as always, made it all work. With everyone under one roof again, we spent a lot of time talking about the business—its history, its current course, and, of course, its future.

Sacha had a lighter academic load than Jason, so he was appointed, as he said, "Chief Rent Collector." It was a little more complicated than that, but in representing the McLean Group, he got to know the mixed bag of tenants occupying our warehouses in East Vancouver. Among them was a stonemason, commercial dry cleaner, gift centre, bakery, electronics giant, mattress factory, elevator test

facility, tools wholesaler, cigarette distribution facility—
and a steady stream of local filmmakers. The technical and
creative challenges of filmmaking appealed to Sacha, and
he began to pay close attention to the growth and needs of
the film industry. I was equally intrigued and began to do a
little homework myself.

British Columbia had been attracting moviemakers for
decades, but in the 1980s, there was an influx of productions that came not just for the great scenery and lower
production costs but for the expertise of local crews. A key
player in developing these crews was an American television writer and producer named Stephen J. Cannell. During his long career, he created such shows as *The Rockford
Files*, *The A-Team*, *Wiseguy*, *Stingray*, and *21 Jump Street*.
In the 1980s, he moved his operation from Los Angeles to
Vancouver to take advantage of lower production costs. He
partnered with Paul Bronfman to build a production facility in North Vancouver, which opened in 1989 and housed,
for the most part, his own productions. There was nothing comparable in Vancouver, though, so our warehouses
remained in high demand by filmmakers who liked the
location.

The more I learned about the industry, the more I liked
it. In 1986, it brought $100 million to British Columbia in
direct spending. In 1996, the year of my health crisis, that
number had increased to half a billion. Those sums were not
the collective totals of production budgets, which were, of
course, much larger. They were sums spent directly in British Columbia on goods and services provided by individuals
and local businesses, whether they were holding a camera,

driving a taxi, selling lumber, or renting a warehouse. I had a couple of non-architectural sketches of a potential production facility drawn up by our real estate group, but they were rudimentary site plans at best with ballpoint pen outlines of ten or twelve big boxes representing sound stages in the middle of the site.

Well, it was an interesting notion but completely impractical from my perspective. Sacha, however, remained interested.

IN THE SPRING of 1998, Brenda, Sacha, and I travelled to Scottsdale, Arizona, to get away from the twofold gloom of our failure to launch Still Creek Village and the Vancouver weather. We stayed in a rental house in a development called The Boulders, and it was there that the idea of Vancouver Film Studios was born. With Still Creek a lost cause, I had decided to sell what I now called the Grandview lands, but the market was bad and the thought of selling them at fire sale prices was more than I could stomach.

Sacha was sitting on the couch and I was engaged in a spirited monologue about zoning constraints when the conversation shifted or, should I say, started. Sacha led the charge. What if we quit banging our heads against the wall trying to get the property rezoned? What if we did something that was outright approved for a change? What if we actually figured out how to build a first-class Hollywood-style film and television studio on our land? How would we finance such a monster? Let's think positively! Let's make this happen! Let's turn this ship around. It was second-generation enthusiasm, but it was infectious and it worked.

Brenda and I went for a walk and ran into a couple of people we knew—the prime minister of Canada, Jean Chrétien, and his wife, Aline, who were vacationing at The Boulders. They invited us to join them for dinner that night. We accepted and agreed that we would follow them in our rental car. Sacha offered to drive, but none of us expected the U.S. presidential-style motorcade we were about to join (which was required for any foreign leader visiting the United States, formally or informally). Sacha's driving instructions were issued by the head of the secret service detachment assigned to the motorcade.

"Keep up and *under no circumstances* are you allowed to stop."

Sacha nodded and Brenda and I buckled up. Surrounded by secret service vehicles, we roared down Scottsdale Road at 130 kilometres an hour, running every red light on the way. What an experience! I think we would be stretching it a bit if we claimed that experience—as unusual and cathartic as it was—sealed the deal for Vancouver Film Studios, but as Sacha wrote later, "There was something in the air that day that gave us the creative energy to make VFS happen, and I can't think of a more fitting way to fire the starter's pistol than dinner with the prime minister of Canada."

WHEN WE GOT back to Vancouver, we did two things: we renamed Northstar International Studios *Vancouver Film Studios*, and we made arrangements to tour every sound stage in Los Angeles, most of which had been built between 1930 and 1950.

Four hundred sound stages later, we knew what we needed to do.

It was time to seek financing. We had a big equity investment in the land and some small first mortgages, but there
was a gap of $20 million between what we had in financ-
ing and what we needed to build the infrastructure and
six new sound stages. We prepared a detailed presentation,
but we knew it would be a tough sell, because the nature
of the film business involved short-term leases. The rents
were good, but the terms were short. Bankers hate uncertainty and the nature of film leases created uncertainty
in spades.

In the spring of 1997, I was at the annual City in Focus
prayer breakfast hosted by Tom Cooper, the organization's
founder and president. I was sitting next to Premier Glen
Clark. I wasn't praying for anything in particular, but I felt
like a prayer was about to be answered when he turned to
me and said, "Tell me about your proposed film studios."

I told him the market was good and the industry would
grow dramatically if we had new and better production
facilities. Local warehouses were bursting at the seams and
no longer met the needs of sophisticated filmmaking.

"It's a clean industry with high levels of employment,"
I said.

He asked if I was experiencing any problems getting the
project off the ground. I explained the financing gap, and
he said, "Show us a proposal and the provincial government will look at a loan."

I went back to the office and worked feverishly to refine
our earlier presentation and make sure our projections
for the growth of the industry were on target. A few days
later, we flew to Victoria to meet with a deputy minister in charge of economic development. Our proposal was

comprehensive and well researched, and when we finished the presentation, the response from the deputy minister was positive.

"You are the only people we've met in the film business who are investing any substantial capital of their own right now."

We quickly advanced to the next level and after a series of additional meetings a loan of $20 million was approved.

In September 1999, we broke ground on the first of six new sound stages, which opened to rave reviews from the film community six months later. Thanks to the generosity of American advisors who shared information with our consultants and architects, we were able to incorporate unprecedented innovations involving construction materials and dimensions, power, and soundproofing. We also decided to lay fibre and build our network backbone at the outset rather than adding it as an expensive afterthought. It was a wise move.

The government's loan was a critical piece without which we could not have built Vancouver Film Studios. I am not a big believer in government financing *business*, but sometimes it makes sense to do so to encourage an industry to develop. It must be done on commercial terms, though, and in the form of loans and not equity. I am happy to report that the loan was repaid four years before it was due and the studios are all now commercially financed. Like all businesses, Vancouver Film Studios is not without its challenges, but the local film industry employs more than fifty thousand people. British Columbia has become a leading production centre for world market films and television series, and we are delighted to have played our part in making it happen.

Today, Vancouver Film Studios is barely recognizable from the construction site of that groundbreaking day in 1999. In addition to twelve modern sound stages, we own and operate Pacific Backlot Services, a production equipment rentals company. We operate Signal Systems, a data-management company that looks after our Cisco phone system, set radios, radio trunk network, and other telecommunication services. We have an experienced and accomplished president and COO, Pete Mitchell, who oversees the management teams responsible for day-to-day operations and marketing of the studios. Pete was formerly the British Columbia film commissioner and has helped us get to know a different industry.

An in-house production company we call Gun Lake Pictures oversees the production of our own corporate videos and other filmmaking projects. A private rooftop helipad is used by our film pilots and aerial coordinators who work in the film division of our helicopter and jet charter company, Blackcomb Aviation.

The obligatory Cape Cod–style gatehouse provides twenty-four-seven security and a warm welcome to our tenants and staff. Production offices and mill spaces are housed in separate buildings throughout the lot. Golf carts traverse the lot and a community garden keeps the local rabbits happy. And threading its way alongside the sound stages and film trucks is Still Creek.

Vancouver Film Studios hosts more than $500 million of productions annually, the majority of which originates from Los Angeles and New York and is destined for world markets, but in 2012, for the first time in more than eighty years, the salmon returned to Still Creek to spawn.

10

Blackcomb Aviation

YOU MIGHT THINK my long association with the railway business would make the shift to aviation an easy one, but the learning curve was steep. There are some similarities, of course. Both are highly regulated transportation services. Both require a complex infrastructure of resources and rigorous safety management systems. Both require access to capital. Both depend on operational efficiencies and regional reputation.

In our case, it started with a phone call from Sacha. He was in his first year at Queen's. He was living in residence and it was about a month into the fall semester. He was taking an arts degree and enjoying campus life. How much was he enjoying it? A parent wonders.

"Dad."

"Yes, Sacha."

"I want to take flying lessons."

"Have you settled on a major yet?"

"Geography."

"What is it you want to fly?"

"Airplanes."

"Oh, I'm all for it, Sacha. It sounds like a great idea, but I know you'll want to tell your mother yourself."

Brenda agreed but with certain cautionary requirements. Go to a good flight school. Train with a good instructor. Learn from the best. I agreed with Brenda's conditions, so with the blessings of both parents, Sacha began the long process of acquiring his commercial fixed wing pilot's licence and commercial helicopter pilot's licence. His love of flight would take a backseat to his studies, but when he returned home to help us market and manage Vancouver Film Studios, a plan began to gel that would lead to Blackcomb Aviation. It would start with an idea to provide the occasional helicopter to local filmmakers for aerial shoots.

THE MAJORITY OF our customers from Los Angeles came (and continue to come) to Vancouver for four reasons—lower production costs, proximity to Los Angeles, crew expertise, and a diversity of film locations that includes some of the most spectacular scenery in the world. To capture that scenery, aerial shoots are common but in 1999 tended to involve a small number of local helicopter companies. By 2002, the demand for helicopters for film shoots and location scouts was growing, but the number of local operators was not.

We decided to establish a small aviation division called Studio Air Group to provide helicopter services for film shoots. We had a helipad installed on the roof of one of our buildings at Vancouver Film Studios and worked with local film pilots who specialized in aerial work. Jason and Sacha were both very keen on this aspect of our business and paid close attention to emerging trends and opportunities. They soon realized that although the demand for helicopters in the film business was significant, it would not provide sufficient revenues on its own. If we were going to move into charter aviation on any significant level, we would need a diversity of services that could provide a balance of revenues by specialty. There were significant barriers to entry, though, and we knew we would not get far without a partner.

The pieces fell into place in 2006, when we partnered with John Morris, founder and owner of Omega Air Corporation, to purchase the Whistler-based Blackcomb Helicopters from Steve Flynn.

We were wise and fortunate in our choice of partner. John Morris was and is an aviation veteran. A pilot to his core, he has airline transport licences for airplanes and helicopters and has been flying since 1976, when he flew float planes off the west coast of British Columbia. In 1980, he moved to the Interior, where he worked as a helicopter pilot, training/check pilot, and, later, base manager for a company active in heavy lift support for construction and offshore oil and gas projects. He then joined Fletcher Challenge Canada Ltd. as general manager and director of flight operations at Vancouver International Airport. He stayed with Fletcher Challenge until 1995, when he established his own company, Omega Air Corporation. John's company provided helicopters, jets, and aircraft management services to other aircraft owners. By the time I met John, his company had a roster of high-profile clients. Their trust in John's judgement and expertise told us everything we needed to know about our new partner. The decision to purchase Blackcomb Helicopters would not have happened without him.

Blackcomb Helicopters was active in tourism, heli-skiing, firefighting, general forestry services, and some utility work. The company also had some very fine film pilots and a long-standing contract with Whistler-Blackcomb. Steve Flynn was ready to retire, but we persuaded him to stay on as our general manager for a few years to see us through the transition.

A year later, we acquired Goldwing Helicopters, a one-helicopter operation in Sechelt, British Columbia, owned by Robin MacGregor, who specialized in the hydro utility and power line sectors. As with Steve Flynn, Robin brought his expertise to the table and assisted us as an advisor while we expanded our pilot pool.

In late 2007, we rebranded our company under the trade name Blackcomb Aviation. Sacha took on the role of CEO, with John serving as president and accountable executive. At the board level, I served as chairman, Jason as secretary, Sacha as vice-chairman, and John as director. Today, Jason is chairman of Blackcomb Aviation and I remain a very interested shareholder.

Working closely with management, we streamlined operations by reducing staff where overlap existed and increasing staffing where it was needed. We expanded our safety management system and quality assurance division and added head-office support in legal affairs, HR, corporate communications, media management, finance, and business development. We invested in a strong bid-writing team and soon began winning some of the largest and most technically demanding bids for aviation services in western Canada. This included the contract for aerial film support for the 2010 Winter Games, which put us on the world stage and was the first of several high-profile dedicated service contracts. It was, to say the least, a pretty good start.

BLACKCOMB AVIATION HAS grown substantially since we joined forces with John Morris in 2006, and we currently operate twenty-six aircraft out of bases in Vancouver, Victoria, Sechelt, Squamish, Whistler, Pemberton, Lillooet, Bridge River Valley, and Phoenix, Arizona. Tourism, heliskiing, mining, oil and gas exploration, general forestry services, firefighting, film, jet charters, independent power projects, and power line construction are all part of our business, and we are the largest provider of services to B.C. Hydro in the province.

Our power line crews have developed technically innovative ways to increase the safety and efficiency of operations in live wire environments. This has included a training facility at our Pemberton base, in partnership with B.C. Hydro and Allteck, which supports practical training exercises for flying-in-the-wire personnel. On the film front, we have a full-time aerial coordinator and have captured a majority share of local film contracts. We have aircraft maintenance services in both fixed and rotary wing divisions at multiple bases and a field unit that services our aircraft in remote locations.

Our customers are diverse, but it is a great tribute to our management and staff that Blackcomb Aviation's mantra (coined by John Morris) of "Safety Respect Value" holds true for everyone. Jet owners may be a different breed than a family of tourists or a heli-ski guide monitoring avalanche conditions or a local community too close to a wildfire or a film crew, but they can all expect the same thing from us: modern aircraft, technical expertise, rigorous safety management, and great customer service.

Moving forward, our intention is to refine and expand our fleet with individual aircraft acquisitions while increasing aircraft utilization throughout North America. With that in mind, we embarked on two ventures in 2012. The first was establishing a presence in the United States to increase helicopter utilization during our shoulder seasons and to support jet charters to the desert southwest during the winter months. Headquartered in Phoenix, Arizona, and operating under Blackcomb Aviation USA, that base is now up and running.

Our second venture was to shore up Blackcomb Aviation's executive team. Our roles within the family were changing and it was no longer possible for Sacha to remain CEO while continuing to provide leadership to our emerging business units. In a similar vein, the demands on John Morris as a pilot, owner, president, and accountable executive were increasing.

It was time to add new strength to the management team and in February of 2013, after an international search conducted by Odgers Berndtson, we hired Jonathan Burke as president and COO of Blackcomb Aviation. In a field of outstanding candidates, Jonathan was a standout. A commercial helicopter pilot with an airline transport pilot rating, he had worked in B.C., Mexico, and the Yukon, where he was co-owner of Yukon Airways. He had an MBA from Athabasca University with post-graduate studies at the University of Pennsylvania's Wharton School and Stanford University's Graduate School of Business. Prior to joining Blackcomb, he had served as vice-president of global market development for Westport Innovations Inc. and held various executive positions in private and public biotechnology companies. And somewhere along the way he had become fluent in three languages: English, French, and Spanish. A few months later, we added Patrick Bradley, an experienced financial professional, as our vice-president of finance. We are now more confident than ever before that the future for Blackcomb is bright with Jonathan and Patrick providing valuable outside leadership to this growing business.

From a helipad on the roof of Vancouver Film Studios, we have grown into an international charter aviation company of stature and reputation. Like the film industry, aviation is not without its challenges, and I admit there are times when Brenda and I look at each other and say "what happened?" In truth, we have only ourselves to blame. When you have two sons with imagination, ambition, guts, and self-discipline—and you go out of your way to encourage them to join the family business—buckle up.

11

"Make room for one another."
BRENDA MCLEAN

Succession Planning

SUCCESSION PLANNING IN a family business is at best problematic, but getting it right is a financial and emotional necessity. Consider the odds. More than 80 percent of Canadian businesses are family owned and operated, but fewer than 30 percent of them survive into generation-to-generation businesses. In our case, succession planning was made somewhat easier by the fact that we had only two sons, both creative, talented, and, in time—well educated.

Jason and Sacha showed an interest in the family business from an early age and had the benefit of learning about it quite literally at the dinner table. Now, I'm not saying we pulled out the balance sheet and swept their homework to one side, but we did talk openly about the business and rarely sugar-coated the challenges we faced during some of the tougher times. This didn't seem to scar them too much, and it certainly gave them a realistic view of the issues involved in running a family business. Sometimes I wondered if we told them too much.

I remember the day Sacha appeared dressed in a blue seersucker suit carrying one of my old briefcases. He was about four years old and dressed for the office. He must have taken the threat of rising interest rates to heart, because he was determined to join me at the office and do what he could to help. We set up a little desk in the corner of my office and tried to make a go of it, but we had to let him go when his nap schedule got out of hand. I think his older brother, Jason, set him straight in a private moment that there was not a lot either of them could do until they were old enough to drive and take over the business. They would have to learn what they could in the meantime and bide their time.

Life went on and they grew up. They were—and are—the best of friends, but as teenagers and young men, their interests and education took them in different directions, which is as it should be. I had complete freedom to choose my own career path in life, as did Brenda. We wanted the same for Jason and Sacha, but we also wanted them to be part of what we were building, so we continued to share information with them about the ups and downs of our business.

Sacha, as mentioned earlier, took a degree in geography and economics at Queen's University and then went to flight school where he learned to fly airplanes and later, helicopters.

Jason took an arts degree in English and political science followed by a law degree at the University of British Columbia. He took time out between his degrees to pursue his love of the outdoors, which included a passion for

mountaineering. Knowing he was at a base camp on Mount Everest or midway up Alaska's Mount McKinley may have kept Brenda awake on occasion, but we knew he was fit, athletic, and very responsible. Jason had grown up skiing, hiking, biking, and participating in all manner of water sports. He was mature beyond his years and understood what he called "expedition behaviour." I remember his explanation of this very clearly on one of his trips home.

"A mountaineering expedition," he said, "is like a bus you can't get off. The trip ends when it ends. Expedition behaviour requires a higher level of civility, diplomacy, and tact. You're on the bus until the trip is over, so you need to bear that in mind when you feel like telling the guy setting up a belay at the top of the ridge he's getting on your nerves."

After law school, Jason articled for a year with a large firm that gave him a taste of what life would be like as a corporate lawyer. It was a good experience, but in 2000, he was offered a job as special assistant in the Office of the Prime Minister of Canada. For the next two years, he travelled the world leading advance teams to Africa, China, the United States, and Europe in preparation for NATO and APEC meetings, G8 summits, and other international trade and diplomatic consultations. It was a different kind of expedition, but Jason's organizational and people skills were tested, refined, and put to good use on the international stage. When he returned home to join the family business in 2002 as executive vice-president, chief legal officer, and corporate secretary, a lengthy title I admittedly modelled after my friend Sean Finn's at CN, we were the beneficiaries of his experience.

Sacha was, by this time, well ensconced in the operational and marketing management of Vancouver Film Studios, and with both sons now working full time in the family business, the structure of our decision-making processes began to evolve.

We had to develop roles that played to our individual strengths. We had to refine and formalize our corporate governance. We had to share equal responsibility for business results and use our collective wisdom in making final judgements on contentious issues. We had to decide as a family at what point our operating businesses would benefit from having a qualified and fully accountable non-family member in the role of president and COO. And last and perhaps most importantly, we had to separate our executive roles from our roles as shareholders and family members.

It wasn't easy, but led by Jason, we embarked on a series of business family education programs separately and as a family that took us from Harvard to the Sauder School of Business. We learned a great deal about ourselves and our business along the way.

Today, Jason is the president and CEO of the McLean Group and Sacha is vice-chair of the McLean Group and president and CEO of McLean Ventures Ltd., his holding company. We have professional non-family managers at Vancouver Film Studios, Blackcomb Aviation, and the real estate group who report to Jason as the CEO. Brenda is vice-chair and I remain the chairman of the McLean Group, and although I work closely with both of my sons, I am happy to say that on a day-to-day basis, they run the show. Jason as CEO focusses on the management teams, financial performance, and executing strategy. Sacha as vice-chair is looking longer term at new business opportunities and how to deliver innovation and—when needed—"entrepreneurial disruption" to our existing enterprises.

We work closely as a family and make decisions on capital spending and operations at quarterly family board meetings. A family business is never without its challenges, but I think our success in transitioning the McLean Group to a second-generation business is tied to five things:

1. Education

Brenda and I have been lifelong education advocates, and health and education are the main themes around our philanthropy. I encourage young people to learn about the world, read widely, and develop critical-thinking skills. Although I have nothing against business education, I've always questioned whether twenty-one-year-olds with commerce degrees have much more to offer a prospective employer than a well-read kid with a degree in classics who took a year to travel around South America. It seems to me that the years between eighteen and twenty-five are as much about learning life skills, self-identity, and judgement as they are about vocational skills and how to perform cost-benefit analysis. As Jason found when he attended Harvard Business School in his thirties, he was a better student when he had a little experience and knew what he hoped to gain from the program. All four of us have derived great insights and intellectual sustenance from our generalist approach to education—bolstered of course by vocational and professional training. You never stop learning.

With that in mind, we attended a family education program at Harvard Business School in 2009 called Families in Business: Generation to Generation. We all stayed in residence and the workload was substantial and enlightening. The Harvard method uses case studies in which endings are withheld to solicit and test solutions put forward by the participants. It makes for suspense and an interesting discussion. In some instances, the cases were presented by video and the individuals featured in them came to class to discuss "their case" in person. We benefited greatly from their generosity in sharing their own experiences.

In addition to case studies, morning meetings were held in which the often-sensitive issues of the families in attendance were discussed in strict confidence with the rest of the group. All of the families had various issues, but some were more complex and difficult to solve than others. By the end of our Harvard course, we felt much better equipped as a family to address the issues facing our own business.

A few years later and a little closer to home, we were featured at a dinner hosted by the Sauder School of Business in support of the families in business education programs at the University of British Columbia. We took our place onstage at various points during the evening for a spirited question and answer discussion hosted by Judi Cunningham, executive director, and Dr. Darren Dahl, senior associate dean, faculty and research, and B.C. Innovation Council professor at the Sauder School of Business. We were particularly pleased that our daughters-in-law, Melanie and Andrea Jane (A.J.), agreed to join us onstage for the final segment of the evening. Their intelligent and witty perspectives on the issues of marrying into a business family were among the highlights of the evening.

2. Communication

Brenda is an advocate of fearless communication. It isn't always easy, but it is remarkable how effective it is when you say what's on your mind without malice or blame. Pressures that build up are released and respect is maintained. Communication is the basis for all good family and business relationships. Another arguably less critical element of communication is the ability to speak and write effectively. These are incredibly valuable skills in business and in life, and we screen for them as best we can in our hiring practices.

3. Respect

We don't always agree, but we treat each other with respect, and since we know each other so well, we try to allow for the discrepancies in our individual perspectives without too much judgement. A sense of humour helps.

4. Friendship

The friendship between Jason and Sacha is central to the success story of our first-to-second-generational transition. At the root of this is a genuine desire to see the other guy succeed—in all aspects of their lives. This is a simple concept but is often lacking in successive generations. Its calming influence over our situation has enabled them to differentiate between their business partnership, their day-to-day executive roles, and their "Bert and Ernie" relationship. Jason has a huge model tugboat in his office by the way, called *Two Brothers.*

5. Inclusion

The marriage of your children is probably one of the biggest challenges in a family business, but if you fail to include your children's partners, it can foster strife and resentment. To avert this, we have a family council that includes our daughters-in-law, Melanie and A.J., and, in time, our grandchildren. Although we are in the early days of the council and it is very much a work in progress, we probably don't meet formally enough. The point is that we are mindful of the critical importance of recognizing all family voices—regardless of their ownership positions. We also believe that the next generation needs to be groomed to be qualified and effective owners, regardless of whether they want to work in the business down the road.

PART THREE

CN

12

"By late 1991, Canadian National's brass knew that, unless they could find a way to switch their railway to a new track, it would hurtle into a tunnel of bankruptcy and never come out."

HARRY BRUCE, *The Pig That Flew: The Battle to Privatize Canadian National*

Back on the Board

THERE IS NOTHING like talk of bankruptcy to clear the field and fill the bleachers. The entrepreneurs move to the sidelines. The referees blow their whistles and the crowd grows loud or silent depending on how much of their own skin is in the game. The rapidly emptying playing field fills up quickly at this point. The lawyers on one side, bankers on the other, and somewhere in the middle, the press and politicians who try to explain what happened without putting on their cleats. Bankruptcy is a human drama like no other. It is, as the Italians say, *banca rotta*—a broken bench.

In the case of CN, broken benches led to its inception as a Crown corporation when it was formed from the amalgamation of financially troubled railways at the end of World War I but in doing so, a second national railway was born. Unlike the privately-owned Canadian Pacific Railway, which preceded it by thirty-eight years, the Canadian National Railway would become known as the "People's Railway." The decades that followed were good ones, especially for people like my father who found opportunity and job security at CN. At the time of my father's retirement in 1963, however, CN was a railroad in transition.

A Crown corporation since 1919, CN had been managed by a series of governments as an instrument of national policy. This was not a highly successful venture from a bottom-line perspective, but in fairness to government, it did ensure CN was well maintained and run somewhat independent of government by a separate board of directors. But since they were all appointed by the government, the government effectively retained control. I am sure the boards of earlier times did their best to keep the railway operating, but by the late 1960s, CN had 120,000 employees and was involved in a multitude of other businesses, including hotels, travel agencies, passenger trains, ships, oil and gas, real estate, package delivery, telephone, telegraph and, yes, trains. Clearly, someone had to get this monster under control. In the meantime, it was a rich source of fodder for political dispute.

CN's struggles interested me as a Canadian, but they did not occupy my thoughts a great deal until 1979 when I was asked by the Trudeau government to join the board. I was grateful my father lived long enough to see his son take a seat in the CN boardroom, but what was meant to be a three-year term stretched to eight, and after eight years, I was weary of Crown corporations. The boy in me would always love trains, but as a lawyer and businessman, I saw things differently. CN, at that time, had too many social and political agendas. It was unlikely to be "hurtled into a tunnel of bankruptcy," but the gravity of its financial situation was painfully apparent.

I stayed on the CN board until 1986, serving under Dr. Maurice LeClair, who was president and CEO during my last four years on the board. Maurice had done a good job under very difficult circumstances, but there had been an election and Prime Minister Brian Mulroney was leading a Conservative government. As a liberal, I thought they should have the right to choose their own directors. Maurice assured me there was no pressure on me to resign, but I knew it was the right thing to do.

So I returned to my life in British Columbia. My sons were at school, the family business was expanding, interest rates were about to start falling, and there was an abundance of new opportunities on the horizon. Despite my best intentions to say no, I would, at various times in the years ahead, serve as chair of the Vancouver Board of Trade, chair of the Canadian Chamber of Commerce, chair of the Duke of Edinburgh's Charter for Business in Canada, co-chair of the University of Alberta's fundraising campaign, chair of the board of Concord Pacific, chair of the board of Coastland Wood Industries, chair of Westech Information System, and proud scoutmaster of the St. George's Scout troop.

CN was never far from my mind, but it was no longer taking up space. It was a seven-year reprieve.

IN THE EARLY spring of 1993, I received a phone call from Jean Chrétien, who was at that time Leader of the Opposition. He asked me to join him for lunch at Stornoway, the official residence of the Leader of the Opposition. I said I would be delighted, and since we had known each other for many years, it was a relaxed and informal lunch. There would be a federal election that fall and during the course of our conversation, he asked if I would consider running for office. This was a game-changing question in every way for me, and had it come earlier in my career, I might have answered differently. But I was nearing the end of a one-year term as chair of the Canadian Chamber of Commerce, which had overlapped with a one-year term as chair of the Vancouver Board of Trade. Once again, I had taken on responsibilities that took me away from my family and my business for extended periods of time and I was anxious to get back to running my family business full time. I was flattered to be asked and sorely tempted to be part of a Chrétien campaign that I knew would put the Liberals back in power, but I had also come to realize that my leadership skills were more suited to business than public office. I would prefer, I said, to help him at some job that had business implications. He was very generous in accepting my reasoning and we ended the discussion on good terms.

On October 25, 1993, Jean Chrétien defeated Kim Campbell and was elected prime minister of Canada. His victory was a major turning point for Canada, as he had a large majority and a mandate to make some fundamental economic changes. He proceeded quickly, sending a clear signal that his government was going to eliminate the budget deficit and begin to pay down the country's debt. To do so would require strong financial discipline and involve cutting not only the growth of government and its services but also its size. He appointed a strong minister of finance in Paul Martin, who went to work with the prime minister's backing.

As part of the process, the government began looking at everything they could do to cut the cost of government and make it more efficient. There would be no sacred cows. It would take many months to determine exactly what major changes needed to be made, and during this time, the privatization of CN was in the rumour mill.

In the late spring of 1994, I received a few calls from friends close to the prime minister asking whether I would be interested in returning to the CN board. I would not be interested if it was to remain a Crown corporation, I said, but should it be privatized, it would have a huge appeal for me.

Rumours became reality a few months later and I rejoined the board in August of 1994 as a director. The chairman at that time, Brian Smith, was also from British Columbia and I knew him well. I also knew that chairing CN was both a full-time job and an order-in-council appointment (as every Crown corporation chair was) that required all of my assets to be put into a blind trust. The role of chair, then, did not appeal to me, because I was not prepared to put all of my assets into a blind trust and I did not need a full-time job. I had one.

A short time later, I received inquiries from some friends in Ottawa to see whether I would be interested in chairing the board if they could arrange to avoid the full-time job and the blind trust. I said I would and at some point later that fall Paul Tellier called me to say that he had been asked to recommend that I be elected acting chairman of the CN board effective December 1, 1994, when Brian Smith's term was up. I accepted the offer and at the next board meeting was formally elected.

And with that, my journey began or, perhaps I should say, resumed. Eleven months later, we closed the largest initial public offering of stock in Canada. It was a 350-day marathon I will never forget and the renewal of a relationship with CN that would last for the next nineteen and a half years.

ONE OF MY FIRST tasks as a director was to chair a board committee to review an offer from Canadian Pacific to buy our eastern lines. We studied it carefully, but our initial instinct was that it was a bad deal for CN and a good one for CP. Instinct doesn't drive the bus, so we arranged to have it analyzed by three separate investment banks: CIBC Wood Gundy acting for the minister of transport, BMO acting for the Privy Council, and Morgan Stanley, which served as a financial advisor to the CN board.

Each of these institutions came to a similar conclusion. It was a great deal for our competitors and a bad one for us. I travelled to New York to meet with our Morgan Stanley analysts, whose conclusion was negative $500 million. The other banks expressed similar misgivings, though to be truthful, one was negative and the other was break even. I knew we were not in business to do either of those things, so the decision to pass was an easy one. The government agreed and the deal was dead.

While I was in New York, I quietly asked several senior Morgan Stanley bankers for their views on Paul Tellier's performance as CEO. With his civil service background, was he the right person to lead a company like CN through an IPO? It was a question on the minds of many and it could not be ignored. I was pleased to hear that the general consensus was that Paul had already proven himself very good at the job and when it came time for the IPO the street would like him. I flew back to Ottawa and met with the prime minister to convey the negative reviews on CP's offer and the positive ones on our CEO. If we were going to do the IPO in eleven months, we would need Paul Tellier's leadership and commitment. We had the right man in place. The prime minister agreed, but as I was leaving the room, he said, "David, be careful."

It was a reminder to me that we needed to take great care in getting this right. The prime minister's decision to sell a revered Crown asset took leadership because it was not a foregone conclusion that it would be successful. To my mind, it was a visionary move. To others, it was not. The prime minister had given me an opportunity to play a significant role in something I believed in as much as he did, and I did not want to let him down. I would indeed be careful.

I left the office that day knowing that my most important task in the months ahead was to gain insights into the strengths and weaknesses of the army of stakeholders who would be my companions or opponents in the marathon ahead. I knew many of them personally and all of them by name or reputation. They were highly competitive individuals, exceptionally accomplished in their respective areas and driven to succeed. I understood them completely. Like them, I had my own strengths and weaknesses. I would need to accept and address my attributes and deficiencies in both areas if I was to lead my side of the team effectively.

DECEMBER 1994 | MONTREAL

The first thing I did after being elected acting chairman was to meet with Paul Tellier at his home in Montreal. Everyone knew Paul was a focussed and hard-working CEO, but what I particularly liked was his openness to any ideas that would move the agenda forward and get the company privatized. This enabled us to have a full and very frank discussion that night about where we wanted to go with CN. The option of privatizing it was now a realistic probability, and we both knew how important timing would be in getting the deal done quickly. The conditions were favourable, but who knew what could happen in a few months? Little did we know.

Looking back, it was one of the best strategic sessions I ever had with a CEO. Paul's background in government had given him extensive knowledge of how government operates. He was fluently bilingual and had a law degree from the University of Ottawa and a post-graduate degree in public administration from Oxford. He had been a civil servant since 1967, and risen up through the ranks to become clerk of the Privy Council and secretary to the Cabinet of the government of Canada. It was the top civil service job in the country. On October 1, 1992, he was appointed president and CEO of CN by Prime Minister Brian Mulroney.

I brought different skills to the table. I spoke bad French, had a law degree from the University of Alberta, and prior to 1985 had juggled a family business with a full-time legal practice. Historically, however, I had been involved at the board level of CN since 1979 and had considerable insight into CN's strengths and weaknesses. I understood the whys and wherefores of its safety record, the importance of keeping railway operations well maintained, the history of its union struggles, and the tremendous value of its pension fund. I also understood what I would need to do as chairman to rebuild the CN board in a way that was gradual and humane but acceptable to the business community and ultimately to the public company's shareholders.

At the time of our meeting, Paul had been actively engaged in two years of cost-cutting, but CN still had a number of peripheral businesses that were not part of the core business of running a railroad. They had divested their hotel assets but still had an oil and gas division, a real estate division, and other business units we would need to dispose of to pay down debt before the IPO. There was plenty to do, not least of which was appointing the investment bankers, preparing the prospectus, and keeping the trains running.

Paul Tellier had been appointed by a Conservative prime minister, and I had been appointed by a Liberal prime minister, but I left that night knowing we would make a good team. Paul knew how to interact with those in power to get the deal done, and I had relationships with the current government at the political level. Paul had been a career bureaucrat and lacked business experience, but his strong work ethic and determination to succeed as CEO made up for these weaknesses. I was a business entrepreneur who lacked government experience, but I understood the needs of the business community. Our job was to maximize the positives of CN, increase its appeal to public shareholders, get the IPO done, and stay out of the minefields. We were committed to doing this right no matter which party was sitting on the government side of the house.

We were also committed to learning from the experience of others. There had been a number of British Crown corporations privatized under the Thatcher government, including British Airways, British Steel, British Petroleum, and British Rail. Paul and I were both planning to attend the World Economic Forum in Davos, Switzerland, that January, so we decided to meet with the CEOs and senior officers of each of those companies while we were in Europe. The forum in Davos, however, would precede those meetings and confirm that among CN's key assets heading into the IPO was its pension fund.

1995 WORLD ECONOMIC FORUM | DAVOS, SWITZERLAND

I had attended the World Economic Forum on a number of previous occasions and knew there was usually a meeting of the chairs and CEOs of the world's major railroads. Of particular interest to me then and on later visits was how many of these railroads did not have great pension plans and how few were well funded. The CN plan had no such deficiencies and one of the main reasons for this was the Swiss-born Tullio Cedraschi, who had it running like a Swiss watch.

Tullio joined CN's investment division in 1968 and in 1977 became CEO and president. When I joined the board in 1979, one of the first things I did was join the investment committee of CN's pension trust funds. I would stay on that committee for an eventual total of twenty-eight years, but at the time of the IPO, I had already seen for myself the positive results of Tullio's careful and thoughtful investment decisions. He invested as if he was investing his own money, but he was also very creative. An example of the latter was his recommendation to the investment committee to purchase the assets of Siebens Oil and Gas in Calgary in the late 1970s. This investment turned out to be one of the best decisions of any pension fund in Canada. The subsequent growth in the value of the assets was excellent and continues to produce an outstanding return to this day.

In Davos, I became acutely aware that our pension fund would be an attractive feature to potential investors as we approached the IPO so long as it did not invest in CN. It would prove a double-edged sword given the tremendous success of our stock after the IPO, but if we were going to steady the nerves of pensioners and employees, the board would need to implement a policy that CN's pension fund would not invest in CN. The wisdom of that decision would serve us well.

JANUARY 1995 | LONDON, ENGLAND

"Beware the golden share."

A golden share is a concept generally floated in government circles in which the government retains a nominal share of a privatized Crown corporation after an IPO, which gives it veto power over certain corporate decisions. The one thing we learned from all of our London meetings—and it was a message that came through loud and clear—was the importance of ensuring that the government did not own any shares of CN after the IPO, golden or otherwise. Everyone we met, from senior corporate officers to investment bankers, stressed the importance of having "clean access." When an IPO was done, they said, the government should have no role except the usual regulatory functions. The size of our IPO, which at approximately $2.3 billion would be the largest ever done in Canada at that time, dictated that if we were to be successful, we would have to have clean access to all capital markets worldwide.

Paul had to leave a day early, but I stayed an extra day for a meeting with a British bureaucrat in Her Majesty's Treasury who had been involved in all of the British privatizations. I was glad I did. Steve Robson was a quiet, unassuming young man in his mid-forties with a dry sense of humour and a quick mind. I liked him from the moment we met and he gave me a great deal of useful ammunition to ensure Canadian government officials would fully understand what it would take to facilitate a successful IPO the size of CN's.

At the end of our meeting, I asked Steve if I could put him in touch with Canadian officials in the Privy Council Office (Paul's old stomping grounds) and the Ministry of Finance. He was agreeable, so I called Paul and said I think I've just found the man we need to brief Canadian officials on what they need to do and *not* do to make the IPO successful.

Paul, through his extensive connections, immediately arranged the follow-up meetings. This was an important step in preparing the way for the IPO. Issues such as a golden share, the government retaining a minority shareholder interest, the importance of a clear regulatory environment, and having open access to global capital markets were all discussed and to a certain extent resolved. There would be additional discussion in the months ahead, particularly about the issue of government shares and deregulation, but we were on the right track, and with Paul Martin's announcement in the House of Commons, it was game time.

FEBRUARY 27, 1995 | OTTAWA

"Today, we are announcing that the Minister of
Transport will initiate steps this year to sell CN."
—PAUL MARTIN, MINISTER OF FINANCE

In anticipation of the announcement, representatives from government and management spent much of December, January, and February adding individuals with good business experience to the board. Doug Young, the minister of transport, did a particularly fine job ensuring good candidates were selected. Getting the right mix of talent and expertise was critical in gaining the confidence of the business community, and there was an abundance of exceptional candidates to consider. It was also a chance to redefine the mandate of the board in keeping with the responsibilities of its future services to an investor-owned company. This would include a clear delineation between the role of the board and the role of management.

Most of us rarely have the chance to create a board from scratch, so this was a golden opportunity. Usually, we are already on a board when we are asked to assume leadership responsibility, whether as chair, lead director, or committee chair, but at CN, we had the responsibility of structuring a new board with a whole new mandate. Accordingly, we wrote the new board mandate with all of the knowledge available to us at the time and in doing so gained a board that would have, at its core, the following features:

1. An independent non-executive chair with a strong mandate to ensure good corporate governance from the start;
2. Independent directors selected for what they could contribute to the board rather than because of their loyalty to an individual CEO; and
3. Independent board committees, which would be especially critical in the areas of human relations and compensation, audit and finance, and corporate governance.

I knew from experience that concurrent with board member selection was board chemistry. Chemistry was not an easy thing to define, but to me it meant (and means) sound judgement, good communication, knowing one another's strengths and weaknesses, open discussions, consensus building, a strong sense of direction, independence of thought and most of all—TRUST.

Board member selection was less ambiguous in some ways but more challenging in others. As CN's newly appointed chairman, careful selection of the new directors was my principal concern. Getting it right would head off many difficult situations and avoid the mistake of adding the wrong person and having to go through the very painful process to correct it. This was one of the worst experiences for a board and especially for its chair, and I wished to avoid it.

In time, we would develop a practice at CN of reviewing our needs for board expertise, geographical representation, and gender balance on a regular basis. These issues would be discussed openly both at our corporate governance committee meetings and through discussions at the board. Suggestions by board members to fill in future gaps in board expertise or representation would be listened to carefully and acted upon as necessary. This kept our board competent and responsive to the company's needs. In the meantime, we had to put that first all-important board together.

We were fortunate in our choices and went with a group of men and women whose collective experience and excellent judgement created business confidence and long-term shareholder value. Many of the original directors would remain on the board for years, and one in particular would emerge as successor when my role as chair came to an end. I'll start with him.

Robert Pace, LLD, was a young lawyer with an MBA and an LLB from Dalhousie University who had worked as Atlantic advisor to Prime Minister Trudeau from 1981 until 1984. He was also a broadcasting entrepreneur who had achieved great success in the radio business. His company, the Pace Group, would later diversify from radio stations into real estate and environmental services, and Robert would go on to become chairman of the board of the Maritime Broadcasting System, chairman of the Walter and Duncan Gordon Foundation, and a director on numerous boards including the Asia Pacific Foundation, Atlantic Salmon Federation, High Liner Foods, and Hydro One. In 2012, Robert received an honorary doctorate from Saint Mary's University, Nova Scotia. Creative, self-disciplined, and strategic, Robert was an outstanding CN director from day one. He chaired the audit committee and, later, the human resources and compensation committee. In 2013, he was unanimously elected vice-chairman in preparation for his appointment as chairman of the board on April 23, 2014. I cannot think of a better successor.

Purdy Crawford was a well-known and very highly regarded corporate lawyer who left the full-time practice of law in 1985 to become CEO of Imasco, Ltd. He had graduated from Dalhousie Law School (now known as the Schulich School of Law) and then taken a master of laws at Harvard Law School. Known to many in the legal community as the "dean emeritus" of corporate law, he had lectured at Osgoode Hall Law School at York University and at the University of Toronto. Purdy was on many corporate boards and had a wealth of experience that would be of great benefit to CN. He would be the recipient of numerous honours and awards in the years ahead, which would include being named an Officer of the Order of Canada in 1996 and a Companion of the Order of Canada in 2007.

Raymond Cyr was president and CEO of one of Canada's largest employers, Bell Canada Enterprises. His journey getting there started in a Montreal orphanage, where he and his four brothers were sent following the death of their mother. Encouraged by Jesuit teachers to get an education, Raymond took a bachelor of applied science at École Polytechnique and in 1958 joined Bell Canada as an engineer. By 1970, he was Quebec City's chief engineer and thirteen years later president of Bell Canada. He became CEO in 1984, chairman of the board in 1985, and president and CEO of Bell Canada Enterprises in 1987. In 1988, he was named an Officer of the Order of Canada. Raymond Cyr was full of courage and common sense.

Maureen Kempston Darkes was president and general manager of General Motors Canada. A lawyer by trade, she joined GM's legal department in 1975 and was appointed general counsel and secretary in 1992. On July 1, 1994, she made business history when she was named the first woman president and GM of General Motors Canada. Maureen went on to become GM's group vice-president and, later, president, GM Latin America, Africa, and the Middle East—and when she left the company in 2009, she had attained the highest operating post ever held by a woman at GM. She would later be named an Officer of the Order of Canada and a fellow of the Institute of Corporate Directors, and be the recipient of the Governor General's Award in Commemoration of the Persons Case (an award created in 1979 to mark the fiftieth anniversary of the famous Persons Case, which ruled that the word "person" included women). Maureen would also be ranked by *Fortune* magazine in 2009 as the twelfth most powerful woman in international business. Maureen was a skillful negotiator and very adept at dealing with multiple stakeholder groups. These abilities would be of great benefit to CN.

Jean Forrest was a distinguished educator and human rights activist who began her career as a teacher in the Manitoba public school system. She later moved to Edmonton, where she served on Alberta's first Human Rights Commission in 1974 and chancellor of the University of Alberta from 1978 to 1982. In 1987, Jean was made an Officer of the Order of Canada in recognition of her service in education, business, and community affairs. Jean left the CN board in 1996, when she was appointed to the Canadian Senate representing Alberta.

Richard Kroft was president of Tryton Investment Co. Ltd., a sophisticated technology company headquartered in Winnipeg, specializing in agricultural research equipment. Richard had a law degree from the University of Manitoba and had worked as executive assistant to the secretary of state for external affairs, Mitchell Sharp, before becoming president of Tryton in 1969. I met Richard's father, Charles Kroft, chairman of the Winnipeg Grain Exchange when we were both on the CN board during the Trudeau government. At CN, Richard would chair our investment committee, which oversees the CN pension fund. He would be made a Member of the Order of Canada in 1997 and, like Jean Forrest, he left CN a few years after the IPO when he was appointed to the Senate.

Denis Losier was an economist, politician, and public servant from New Brunswick. He was president and CEO of the Assumption Mutual Life Insurance Company when he joined the CN board in 1995 but had already served two terms as an MLA and cabinet minister in Premier Frank McKenna's government. Denis was minister of fisheries and aquaculture and minister of economic development and tourism. He was later appointed a member of the Security Intelligence Review Committee of Canada and as such became a member of the Privy Council. In 2011, he would be named a Member of the Order of Canada and be awarded an honorary doctorate in business administration from his alma mater, the University of Moncton. At CN, Denis would do an outstanding job chairing our audit committee.

Dr. Edward Neufeld was former executive vice-president and chief economist at the Royal Bank of Canada and, prior to that, assistant deputy minister of finance in Ottawa. An exceptional analyst and communicator of complex information, Ed had a doctorate from the London School of Economics and had written extensively on the history, challenges, and future of Canadian financial and banking systems. He would later chair the C.D. Howe Institute's Financial Services Research Initiative.

Cedric Ritchie was former chairman and CEO of Scotiabank and widely recognized as one of Canada's top bankers. His fifty-year career with the bank started in 1945, when he was hired as a teller at a small local branch in Bath, New Brunswick. Rising up through the ranks, he was named president and CEO in 1972 and, two years later, chairman. He was made an Officer of the Order of Canada in 1981 and in 2000 was inducted into the Canadian Business Hall of Fame. Cedric Ritchie was a fox—very clever and brimming with experience and good judgement.

THESE WERE MEN and women of great depth and business acumen, and it was because of them that CN's board of directors was so quickly recognized as one of the most impressive boards in Canada. In partnership with management and government, we were ready to prove the doubters wrong. CN might be "a pig with lipstick" in the eyes of the naysayers, who promised they would buy stock "when pigs flew," but for those of us with better vision, the pig was on the runway.

With our board in place, it was on to the bankers. They were a different tribe with different rules, but first we would have to deal with a union strike.

13

"Can you really explain to a
fish what it's like to walk on
land?"

WARREN BUFFETT

Strikes, Banks, and Other Showdowns

WITH APOLOGIES TO my late father, a union steward of great
integrity and commitment, CN as a Crown corporation had
a history of giving in to union demands to the extent that if
you worked for CN for seven years, you effectively had a job
for life. This created a sense of entitlement that, over time,
fostered an unproductive and inefficient work environment.
This badly needed to be corrected, so the scene was set for a
strike. With the IPO looming, we had to be strong and the
government had to get the solution right.

In the past when a railroad went on strike, the government ordered them back to work under compulsory arbitration. The arbitrators, however, being a representative
of labour, management, and a "neutral" chair, too often
tried to satisfy both sides by splitting everything down the

middle. We could not afford this type of solution, as jobs for life were not a viable option in a privatized company.

Paul Tellier and I discussed the strategy we would need to implement if we were to resolve the impending strike properly. We decided the key was to ensure the arbitrators looked at our competitors in the United States for comparables. We then went to work on the government, convincing them to give the arbitrators strict instructions to look at U.S. railways in resolving the dispute.

MARCH 18, 1995 | MONTREAL

On the morning of March 18, the Brotherhood of Maintenance of Way Employees commenced strike action at CN. At 2:15 PM EST, the Brotherhood of Locomotive Engineers and the United Transportation Union began strike action at CN and VIA Rail. At 11:30 PM EST, CN's assistant vice-president Terry Lineker advised Canadian Auto Workers national president Buzz Hargrove that all members of the CAW on CN Rail were locked out and that all terms, conditions, and benefits had been suspended.

I knew from personal experience there were good people on both sides of the dispute, but we were eight months away from the mother of all yard sales and the strike had to end quickly. I did not feel guilty about the steps we were taking to privatize CN because I knew they were necessary, but I understood the effect our decisions were having on CN employees and their families because I had been a member of one of those families.

As we hoped, the government ordered the unions back to work and set terms of reference for the arbitrators that required them to take into account the competitive landscape and the economic viability of CN. The unions were instructed to have the arbitration completed in three months, so it was time for CN to settle on their choice of arbitrator. Paul favoured a prominent lawyer in Montreal. It was an excellent choice, but I knew Paul's candidate was a very busy guy and thought we would do better with someone who could give us more attention.

"How about Peter Gall?" I said. "He's a labour lawyer in Vancouver, a Harvard graduate, and very good at what he does. He's not confrontational, but at the end of the day, I think he'll be respected and influential."

Paul agreed to meet with him, so the next day Peter flew to Montreal. Paul called me after the meeting and said he wanted to go with Peter Gall. This was one of the things I liked best about Paul. He was decisive and not easily dissuaded, but he was a good listener and flexible in adjusting his opinion if he thought it was right for the deal.

The government selected a judge to act as chair, and the arbitration got underway. The judge, George W. Adams of the Ontario Court of Justice (General Division), was an experienced and even-handed man with a good dose of common sense. The arbitration went through the usual stresses and strains on both sides, but in the end, the right decision was made and jobs for life were gone.

Many of the major decisions made during this period of time—particularly those pertaining to the labour climate, the structuring of the company, and the regulatory framework—were decisions that involved the ability to influence people to move in the right direction at the right time. When it came time to appointing the bankers, however, we would take a different approach.

The minister of transport wanted to proceed quickly and have the government appoint the three lead bankers, but many of us were uncomfortable with this approach. There was no question about the competency of the three institutions proposed, but this was the largest IPO in Canadian history and we had to protect the process from any accusations of favouritism. A week after strike action was announced in Montreal, I flew to Ottawa to meet with the prime minister to pitch a slightly less conventional plan. It was a short meeting with an aide in attendance. Appointing the bankers was a critical step and, like the strike, we had to take care in making good decisions. When the prime minister asked what I had in mind, I had my answer ready.

"A beauty contest," I said. "We need to interview a much wider group of national and international investment bankers. We can't make recommendations to your government on which institutions will do the best job if we don't take the time to ask them. Let's give them a chance to show us what they can do for CN."

The prime minister approved the plan. When I left his office, I headed to the airport for a flight to Toronto, where I had another round of meetings. I decided to hire an airline limousine at the airport, as I would be pressed for time and wanted to get back to Vancouver that night. When I emerged from my last Toronto meeting, the driver was waiting for me. He looked worried.

"Are you Mr. McLean?"

"Yes."

"Your office tracked you down," he said. "There's a message for you to call Minister Young in Ottawa."

"Thanks."

"Right away."

The driver seemed determined that I do this immediately and perhaps under his supervision, but I asked him to take me to the airport instead.

"Aren't you going to call the minister?" he said.

"I'll call him from the airport."

"Well, don't forget," he said, and off we went.

By the time I got to the airport, I was in a sufficient state of paranoia that I went looking for a pay phone far away from listening ears. Perhaps my beauty contest had backfired. It was getting late, but the minister picked up the phone right away and without preamble said the prime minister had filled him in on "the beauty contest" and given it his approval. I had no way of knowing whether the minister was pleased, but of course he respected the prime minister's authority, so the pageant was on and a few weeks later I sat down with Paul Tellier and Michael Sabia to compile a list of contestants.

MICHAEL SABIA WAS senior vice-president of corporate development at that time and, later, our chief financial officer. Like Paul, he had a razor-sharp mind and had risen up through the civil service to become an accomplished senior bureaucrat. Michael was a Yale graduate, a brilliant strategist, and a workaholic, even by the standards of the rest of us. With our list of beauty contestants in place, we contacted the senior officers at each institution with an invitation to prepare and present a proposal at our Ottawa offices.

We set aside several days to listen to proposals. The Canadian institutions included RBC Dominion Securities,

BMO Nesbitt Burns, CIBC Wood Gundy, Scotia McLeod, TD Securities, Gordon Capital, Richardson Securities, and a few others. The main non-Canadian banks were Goldman Sachs, J.P. Morgan, and Morgan Stanley. After several exhausting days of listening, taking notes and asking questions, Michael, Paul, and I met to confer. We were pleased and somewhat relieved to discover that we all felt Goldman Sachs had, by far, made the best presentation. They had also done most of the recent railway stock issues in the United States, with the exception of one done by Morgan Stanley (in which Morgan Stanley owned a big piece of the railway). This was an interesting development because Morgan Stanley had been CN's investment advisor for many years and as a result, they should have had the inside track. What went wrong?

They sent the same team of executives we had met on many previous occasions, none of whom were the senior officers of the bank. Their presentation was a bit tired and they made the mistake of making inaccurate and inappropriate comments about the competition. This was fatal to their presentation.

In the end, we recommended to the government they appoint Goldman Sachs as our lead U.S. banker and BMO Nesbitt Burns and Scotia McLeod as our lead Canadian bankers. Goldman's rail analyst, Craig Kloner, worked incredibly hard to expose the issue to major investors who had done well on previous rail deals. Much of the credit for being nine times oversubscribed on the night of the IPO was due to Craig Kloner's work, credibility, and reputation.

It would be my job to phone all of the banks and relay our decisions, but before I could do that, we had to allocate

the fees. When the Mulroney government was in power and privatizing Air Canada and other Crown corporations, RBC Dominion Securities often received the lead position on most issues, but we wanted to spread the fees around to ensure all of the banks would be motivated to work hard on the issue.

RBC had received 25 percent of most of the other issues, so it was suggested our three lead banks get 15 percent each for a total of 45 percent among Goldman Sachs, BMO, and Scotia McLeod. The next line of five banks, RBC Dominion, CIBC, TD Securities, Richardson's and Gordon Capital would get 10 percent each. We would then spread the balance of 5 percent among a number of smaller regional banks. The total fees were about $80 million, so to put it into perspective, 1 percent was worth $800,000. This was not small change in an IPO that would be nine times oversubscribed. Paul and Michael agreed with these allocations, as did the government, who had final say.

I called all of our pageant winners personally, and they were all pleased with their allocations. When I called Tony Fell, CEO at RBC Dominion, he was surprised they were getting anything, so when I told him he was getting 10 percent he was thrilled. We had a very pleasant conversation, and just as I was about to hang up, he said, "Oh, David, can we be on the left side?"

The left side is the lead banker for that group and is a very prestigious positioning. I think Tony may have thought since I was not a Bay Street guy, I might have just fallen off the turnip truck. When I was first appointed, I heard there were rumours on Bay Street about this guy from Vancouver who didn't know anything about capital markets. In truth,

I came to CN with little experience in investment banking, public companies, and the weird and wonderful ways of stock markets and securities commissions, but the fundamentals I had learned in law school and business stood me in good stead.

Still—the left side, Tony? I could feel the weight of the chip on my shoulder as Tony waited for my response.

"Tony," I said, "you just got 10 percent. Don't push your luck."

He laughed and thanked me for the 10 percent. Tony Fell was a true gentleman, and I couldn't blame him for trying to better their position. As for me—well, I had a tendency to huff and puff on occasion and needed to keep my cool.

The day after the bankers were announced, I received a call from a senior officer of Morgan Stanley who was shocked to learn they had not been chosen and asked if I could enlighten him so that they could learn from the experience. I thought very carefully before replying.

"Tell your guys to be careful before knocking the opposition."

He thanked me for being so frank and said he would deal with the situation.

MAY 25, 1995 | CALGARY

"Have I mentioned the golden share?"

It was six months after our meetings in London and the golden share continued to hover over the IPO like Marley's ghost. We knew from our London meetings that a key element in succeeding with the IPO was to persuade the government to relinquish any thought of owning shares after the IPO. The privatizations done by the Mulroney government had had mixed success, because they continued to own a block of stock and this was not welcome to the investment community. Petro-Canada was a good example, its stock languishing for many years because of the government overhang.

We also needed to persuade the government to complete deregulation of the Canadian rail industry, which had suffered in the past from too much interference in normal commercial transactions. Both of these issues had been discussed at previous meetings, but they had not been resolved. We were now six months away from the IPO and we had to assure investors that the IPO would be clean of government overhang and that deregulation of the rail industry would be completed.

I felt it was time to communicate directly with the prime minister about this, so I put in a request for a private meeting. Such meetings are not common, as there is generally a staff member present, but I successfully set up a meeting on May 25. The prime minister had a meeting in Calgary with Alberta premier Ralph Klein and could give me an hour of his time beforehand.

I arrived early and the prime minister joined me a few minutes later. As always, he got straight to the point and encouraged me to do the same. We had a very candid discussion about the outstanding issues and the ways in which they would handicap the success of the IPO. We needed access to world markets and, in order to get it, the government had to sell all its shares and continue with the deregulation of the rail industry. Everyone knew deregulation was underway and could not be done before the IPO, but we needed a signal that the government was serious about completing it in a timely manner.

The meeting ended on a positive note, but the prime minister was clear in cautioning me that the final decision on golden shares and deregulation would lie elsewhere. "David, I respect your advice on these matters," he said, "but I have a Cabinet and backbench MPs that will need to be convinced you are right."

I believe I then made some vaguely inappropriate comment about the prime minister of Canada being persuasive enough to sell refrigerators in Antarctica, which he kindly ignored.

Our hour was up and the meeting was over, but a few weeks later we received word that the government was committed to selling all of their CN shares. There would be a limit of 15 percent on any one shareholder to ensure the company was more likely to remain in Canada, but there would be no restriction on the nationality of shareholders. The government also made it clear that deregulation of the industry would be completed. It was the best possible news and the removal of a couple of huge road blocks in our path. Now if we could just get the bankers to behave.

A FEW MONTHS before the IPO closed, discussions were held involving an increase of fees and allocation of shares to Canadian bankers. Certain CN officers and government officials were considering the possibility of increasing the underwriter fees to ensure a successful IPO. I was not one of them. The fees on the IPO were in excess of $80 million. The three top-line Canadian investment banks stood to make 15 percent of that amount—$12 million each—and they wanted more? In my view, they were being well rewarded and would earn handsome commissions trading the stock after the IPO. I said I would have a quiet word with the bankers. But first, I would be making a quiet phone call.

I had retained a retired advisor in Vancouver who had spent his career working in the investment industry and knew all the players. I trusted him and appreciated his straightforward views. "Oh, this is typical with these investment bankers," he said. "They're a greedy bunch and will always ask for more. It won't affect the issue at all. They're just trying to see how smart you are."

The irony was that the firm that had really done the important work in creating a market for our stock was Goldman Sachs and they were not asking for more. In fact, their representative, Mark Tercek, was our most impressive advisor, to say nothing of Craig Kloner's extraordinary performance.

I invited the senior officers from two of the investment banks to join me for breakfast in my hotel suite the following week. I'm glad I waited, because in the next few days, I received reports they had been lobbying Ottawa and meeting with officials from finance and the Privy Council. Although we had fought hard for months for the freedom to sell the stock to the world capital markets, they now felt we should set aside a larger number of shares to be sold in Canada. The truth was they had suddenly woken up to realize

Goldman Sachs had done a great job in creating a market in the U.S. and they might not make as big a fee if more stock was sold in the U.S.

The meeting started out quite cordially, but as we got to the end of breakfast and my blood sugar stabilized, I cut to the chase.

"I've heard that you're not happy with the fees you're going to earn on the IPO."

"Oh, we are not unhappy," was the response. "We just feel we should be paid an additional work fee since most of the work was done in Canada."

"I see. So you want some extra fees because you worked so hard in Canada?"

Yes, they said, yes on both counts.

I said, "Well, let me make it clear. There will be no additional work fees, and if you're not happy, let me know and I'll call Tony Fell at RBC Dominion to see if he'd like to fill your spot."

They back-pedalled fast. They were not unhappy. They just felt they should be fairly paid for what they'd done. I would like to say that the following speech came forth as calmly and articulately as I've written it below, but to the best of my recollection, it went something like this: "You are being very well paid. This issue will be oversubscribed and most of the credit for that goes to Goldman Sachs. They created the deep market with their worldwide contacts, so if anyone should be paid more, it's probably them, but they are not asking for more."

I called Paul Tellier and said the meeting with the bankers had gone well.

IT IS MARCH 9, 1996. *It has been four months since the IPO and six months since I had "a quiet word" with the bankers.*

I have been invited to speak to the graduating law class at my beloved alma mater, the University of Alberta. It is an invitation that fills me with great joy. I begin with a tribute to my mentors Dr. Smith and Dean Bowker and a reassurance to students who are not in the top third of the class that their future success depends on more than their marks in law school. The fact that you have graduated, I tell them, shows you have capacity, but it will be your ability to deal with people, your maturity of judgement, and your depth of determination that set your course ahead.

I talk about the IPO and the "depth of determination" that led to its success. How did we do it? We looked at previous privatizations and learned from their mistakes. We prepared our course of action just as we would an assignment—piece by piece until it all came together.

And then I talk about reputation. Your reputation, I say, will become a critical factor in your future success. If you are too tough, you will ultimately pay a price, and if you are a pushover, the word will get around and you will have only fools for clients. But if you are fair but firm and listen to the real needs of your clients—which are often not the ones they articulate when they first come to see you—you will succeed.

Fair but firm, I say again, and then I read them a poem on success by Ralph Waldo Emerson.

14

"Rest is not idleness."
SIR JOHN LUBBOCK

Talking Sticks and Referendums

AS WE REACHED late August, the tension at the CN office in Montreal was rising. Paul Tellier, Michael Sabia, and Claude Mongeau had the focus and self-discipline to carry crushing workloads, but it came with an intensity that was as hard on others as it was on them. I decided to step in but knew I would need to tread carefully, because I was encroaching on management's turf.

I had a couple of things in mind. First, that we "make" Michael Sabia take a holiday to fortify his prodigious energies for the push ahead and, second, that we engage the board, key advisors, and selected management in a chemistry-building exercise. The former would involve the art of persuasion. The latter would involve a train ride and a talking stick.

With the Quebec referendum looming on the fall horizon, I felt we needed to get away from eastern Canada. We needed perspective and we needed to regain a connection with the value of CN. The sheer volume and complexity of our individual responsibilities ran the risk of isolating us from the strength of the team. Perhaps I was channelling the Scout camps of my youth, but I truly believed in the value of group chemistry and knew we would need it as much as we would need our individual superstars if we were to complete the IPO.

"I want to bring the board out west for our next board meeting," I said to Paul, "along with some of our key advisors, bankers, and senior officers. We'll all meet in Kamloops and then travel to Vancouver on CN's business train cars. It will give everyone an opportunity to experience the railroad they are selling in action. And it will provide a social setting for everyone to relax and get to know each other better."

Paul understood where I was coming from but had serious misgivings about the timing of a trip west. Michael in particular, he cautioned, would never take a break.

"He's too involved in the process," he said.

"We all are," I said. "That's the problem."

Paul may not have been a Queen's Scout, but he saw the value in my proposal and gave me the go-ahead. I then called Michael and asked him out for lunch. We went to a restaurant in a relaxed setting away from the office. We had a pleasant conversation over lunch, and when we were almost finished I said, "Michael, you are immersed in what you are doing which is critical to our success but this is a marathon not a sprint. We need you refreshed and ready for the final leg of the race. Maybe you should take a break."

"Mr. McLean, you can't ask me to do this. We'll lose the momentum."

It was on to round two. One of the benefits of being slightly insensitive is the ability to keep swinging.

"Michael," I said, "I promise you will not lose the momentum. In fact, when you come back relaxed and refreshed, you'll sprint across the finish line. Now let's talk about where you and your family would like to go. How about a trip to Lake Louise? You could spend a week there and then come out to the coast. We're having a board meeting in Vancouver with our advisors in a couple of weeks and it would be great if you could be there."

He said he had always loved the mountains of Alberta. Maybe a week of hiking and relaxation wouldn't be such a bad idea.

SEPTEMBER 1995 | VANCOUVER

A few weeks later, Michael and his wife arrived in Vancouver for the CN dinner, which Brenda and I decided to host at our home. It was a wonderful evening. The train trip from Kamloops to Vancouver with the board and other senior CN officers had gone as well as I'd hoped, and by the time we all gathered for dinner, everyone was relaxed and enjoying one another's company. They say that tension reveals who we think we should be but relaxation reveals our true natures. The men and women present that night were all ambitious, self-disciplined, and highly accomplished individuals, but in a relaxed setting away from the pressures of

IPOS and referendums, workloads were set aside and energies were restored.

That summer, my son Jason had been working for the Canadian Coast Guard at Alert Bay, which is a small village on an island just off the northern tip of Vancouver Island. Alert Bay is in traditional Kwakwaka'wakw territory and I asked Jason to commission a talking stick from one of the local artists.

I wanted it to feature some of the animals found on the CN line from Jasper to Vancouver—bears, wolves, eagles, and, of course, salmon. It arrived a few days before the dinner, so I called a friend who kept an eye on our Bowen Island property and asked whether he could find a fallen cedar tree and cut a large round from its base. He delivered it the next day and we drilled a hole in the centre into which we placed the talking stick. I then had a plaque made and mounted on the base. I felt like I deserved a merit badge.

A talking stick is a symbol of authority in the aboriginal community. It is used to maintain an atmosphere of respect in meetings by ensuring that the discussions are not dominated or interrupted. The person who holds the talking stick is the only person entitled to talk, but the stick is passed from person to person to ensure everyone's opinion is heard.

I have always loved the symbolism and spiritual significance of the talking stick, so at the end of the dinner, I presented it to Paul Tellier on behalf of the CN board. I told him that as the main spokesman for CN, he would be doing a lot of talking between now and the end of November, not least of which was the CN road show, which would be heard in twenty-six cities on two continents by some of the toughest business audiences in the world.

"This symbol of respect," I said, "will give you the positive energy you need to finish the road show and the IPO with style and grace."

The evening ended on a high note. We had many long days ahead, but we knew that our principal responsibility was to stay focussed and remain positive. That would, of course, become easier if Canada survived the Quebec referendum.

IT WAS TOUGH enough putting together the largest IPO in Canadian history, but having a referendum about the future of Quebec's place in Canada a month before it closed was salt in our wounds. In late September, I met with the prime minister and spoke to him about the referendum.

"In the event the referendum goes the wrong way," I said, "I think we can still close the IPO, but we need you to give us some time to do it."

He said he could give us a month. We didn't need it. The federalists defeated the separatists in a margin for the history books: 50.58 percent of Quebecers voted to stay in Canada and 49.42 percent voted to leave. We had dodged another bullet and perhaps our most significant one. It would have been very difficult selling a national railway if the nation selling it was on shaky ground.

We were now thirty days from the IPO.

Everyone had "done their job," as Coach McIntosh would say, and the market liked the deal, but the government was getting a lot of heat from the press and others in light of the strong demand for our stock. It was important that a sufficient number of Canadians be allowed to buy the IPO or they would feel left out, but exactly what number was sufficient? Not everyone agreed on the answer to this question. I received a call from the Prime Minister's Office expressing concern over this. Although the majority of demand had been created in the U.S., we understood the importance of ensuring that Canadians had access and proposed we allocate 20 percent to the Canadian retail market, 40 percent to the Canadian institutional market, and the remaining 40 percent to world institutional markets (which meant mostly the U.S.).

The Prime Minister's Office agreed with these numbers subject to approval from the minister of finance, Paul Martin, who also agreed. I then called Paul Tellier to advise him we had a deal, but Paul did not love the numbers because he felt more should go to the U.S. This was understandable and in keeping with Paul's vision to transform CN into the best freight railroad in North America. And he wasn't the only one who disagreed with the numbers. Our U.S. bankers wanted at least 50 percent and some of our Canadian bankers wanted up to 70 percent. Obviously, we thought the numbers were fair and reasonable or we would not have proposed them, but there would be a final rally from all those opposed five days before CN was sold to the underwriters. It would be a contentious meeting at an airport hotel on Remembrance Day.

NOVEMBER 11, 1995 | MONTREAL AIRPORT
HILTON HOTEL

It was a Saturday afternoon and the attendees included Paul Tellier, Michael Sabia, and myself from CN; senior representatives from our lead bankers both north and south of the border; Moya Greene and Doug Young from the Ministry of Transport; and David Dodge, who was deputy minister of finance. The location of the meeting had been selected to accommodate Doug Young, who was flying to China on government business later that day, but unfortunately the plane that went to pick him up in New Brunswick landed at the wrong airport. This delayed the start of the meeting by almost an hour, and by the time he arrived, tensions were high and nobody had brought a talking stick. Fortunately, Paul Martin chaired the meeting, kept the agenda moving forward, and made short shrift of unproductive acrimony.

The purpose of the meeting was to finalize any last-minute details and put the numbers to bed once and for all. Nobody was happy with their share and fought hard for more. Things became heated and a few things were said about greed, politics, ownership, and history that did not play well on Remembrance Day. There was agreement, however, on one key point: CN's stock offering was likely to be successful.

NOVEMBER 28, 1995

"Some pig!"—E.B. WHITE

In the end, all of the late nights and disagreements seemed unimportant when the biggest IPO in Canadian history went off without a hitch. Many of us thought the stock would go to a small premium after the IPO and the Canadian retail market would then sell, making a modest profit, at which point the U.S. institutions would buy more. This prediction proved correct and within a few days most of the Canadian retail market had sold and the U.S. institutions owned close to 60 percent of the issue, having paid a 10 percent premium to do so. Canadian institutions took up the 40 percent allocated to them, but it was surprising to many observers that a number of our large national pension funds and money managers did not initially buy our stock.

Some sat on the sidelines for years while the stock proceeded to increase in value—more than 220 percent in the first five years alone. In fact, many of these institutions bought stock only after CN had five to six years of solid earnings and growth. They still did well, but they would have done better if they had bought in year one. To put it into perspective, if you had bought one share of CN at the IPO, and accounting for four stock splits, your stock would have appreciated almost twenty-six times in eighteen years with the stock trading at the end of 2013 at around CAD$60. Or if you prefer the big numbers, our market capitalization has gone from about $2.3 billion when we closed the IPO to more than $50 billion today.

Of course, one of the large national pension funds who did not buy our stock was our own, but that decision was made prior to the IPO. Employees could invest personally and I hope for their sakes they did, but later, when we saw the tragedies in the U.S. when companies that had large pension funds with huge positions in their own stock ran into trouble (as many did after 2008), the board was reassured that they had made the right decision. For those of us on the board, however, the purchase of stock was not an option. It was a requirement.

above The McLean Group's award-winning heritage renovation of The Landing in 1985 was a labour of love.

top left The gatehouse at our film and production facility, Vancouver Film Studios.

bottom left A 2011 photo of Blackcomb Aviation's owners, *(left to right)* Jason, me, Sacha, and our partner, John Morris.

above Sacha is a commercial helicopter and jet pilot and family lead on our move into charter aviation.

top left A second-generation family business needs second-generation leadership. In 2011, Jason was appointed CEO of the McLean Group.

bottom left In 2011, we were invited to share the story of our family business at the Family Legacy Dinner hosted by the UBC Sauder School of Business. *(Left to right)* Sacha, Brenda, Jason, me, Judi Cunningham, and Dr. Darren Dahl.

above Chairman of the CN board (1994–2014).

above With my good friend Sean Finn, executive vice-president, corporate services, and chief legal officer at CN.

top right Claude Mongeau, president and CEO of CN *(centre)* with David McLean, chairman *(left)*, and Robert Pace, vice-chairman *(right)*.

bottom right For leadership on the basketball court, look to my friend Steve Nash, who presented me with his jersey at the game between Canada and China. Canada won!

top I have received four honorary doctorates of law, but the one from my alma mater, the University of Alberta, holds a special place in my heart.

above The 2013 CN board: *(front row, left to right)* Donald Carty, Michael Armellino, Maureen Kempston Darkes, Edith Holiday, Charles Baillie, and Denis Losier; *(back row, left to right)* James O'Connor, Robert Pace (vice-chairman), Claude Mongeau (president and CEO), David McLean (chairman), Ambassador Gordon Giffin, Hugh Bolton, and Edward C. Lumley.

It is fundamental to every board that they focus on the creation of solid long-term shareholder value. In essence, they are the trustees of the shareholders' investment, so respect for that investment is paramount in decision making. It all comes down to good judgement and a belief that you will make better decisions if you have some skin in the game. Each decision can then become an honest test of the question "Would I invest my money in this manner?" It sounds simple, but it always amazes me when I hear about boards that seem to have forgotten about the people who invested the money to create the business in the first place— the shareholders.

I am proud to say that the CN board has a minimum share ownership requirement of USD$900,000, which must be met within five years of joining the board, and USD$1,410,000 for the board chair. The average dollar value of the share ownership of each director at CN has increased over the years, and at the time of this writing, our directors, excluding the CEO, have an average shareholding of well over $10 million per board member. This is probably the highest investment per board member of any board in Canada and shows the tremendous confidence we have in the company.

But the decision to privatize CN was not made to reward its shareholders, directors, employees, and pensioners. The decision to privatize was made because the country needed an efficient, well-managed railway that was focussed on providing critical transportation of goods to market. It was made because Canada is a huge exporter of raw materials and much of our GDP is best served by rail. It was made because CN's struggling performance as a Crown corporation could no longer be left for the next government to fix, defend, or ignore. It was time to address the issues and do something about them. In taking action when they did, the government ensured CN would survive and prosper and, in doing so, return huge financial benefits to Canada.

Not only did the government of Canada receive a cheque for $2.3 billion from the IPO, it began—for the first time in seventy-six years—to receive income tax payments from the now-privatized company. This was never the case when CN was a Crown corporation, so perhaps there is some truth to the maxim "Why own the cow when you can get the milk for free?"

Having seen CN operate as both a Crown corporation and a public company, I have no hesitation in saying that the country is far better off with a privatized CN. It is the world's most efficient rail transportation company and has clearly given our country a tremendous competitive edge.

15

"The reward for work well
done is the opportunity to do
more."
JONAS SALK

New Tracks

THERE WAS NOT much time to celebrate the success of the IPO, because the company was immediately engaged in a search for new sources of revenue. I have always felt that growing revenue is a laudable objective, so long as they are revenues that result in income on the bottom line. CN management was well aware of that reality and knew they would be compensated for achieving results based on that objective if we could persuade them to accept it.

In early 1996, after discussions with our human resources committee, we offered Paul Tellier a modest bonus for the tremendous work he had done on the IPO. He chose to take only half the amount offered, because he did not want it to appear he was taking advantage of the government. The board felt he was entitled to the full amount, but Paul was never motivated solely by money. First and foremost, he was interested in high-quality and efficient performance, and that included his own. This was very much reflected in the successful growth of CN under Paul's tenure as CEO.

At the board level, we had other duties, and my job was to get the board engaged in active oversight of this newly hatched public company. One of those tasks was to give our committees strong mandates to oversee the policies set by the board. This included our compensation committee, which was later renamed the human resources and compensation committee. Purdy Crawford chaired this committee and established sound principles upon which management (then and in the future) would be compensated. We wanted management to be strongly motivated to build solid value for our shareholders. This would require both short-term and long-term methods of compensation. Purdy, in partnership with his committee and an outside consultant, established a compensation plan that would reward strong performance fairly if, and *only* if, specific targets were met. This would ensure that CN's compensation plan was fair to shareholders.

Since I am neither an accountant nor an MBA, my view of compensation was based on my experience in business. I may not have been the most sophisticated guy, but I was very concerned with basics. I had a simple formula involving five "tests" that needed to be met by management to make a company successful:

1. First, was cost control, and CN clearly had that one right, but it was critical to keep our eye on the ball and not ease up.

2. Second, we needed to generate new sources of revenue but ensure that it was revenue going to the bottom line.
3. Third, I felt that any company worth its salt had to produce a return on capital sufficient to justify a return greater than its cost of capital.
4. Fourth, we had to produce a return on equity that, to my simple way of thinking, would be at least double the return we expected on capital.
5. When the first four tests were met, the fifth test—which in my view is the real test of a mature company—was "free cash flow." I always saw the fifth test in terms of a simple question: "When you've paid all your bills, how much cash is left uncommitted?" The answer to that question is a good indicator of how you are doing.

CN's compensation system eventually embodied all of these tests, and I remember when the first four were met and the conversation turned to free cash flow. Our first target was $250 million and management came in with $400 million. We never looked back and each year our focus on sustainable free cash flow has intensified. Even today, with the headwinds of cash taxes and requirements to do extra funding to our pension fund, we are still able to generate substantial free cash flow.

The board is understandably proud of CN's financial performance in this area, because it takes a special focus to make it happen. Our management teams, led at various times by Paul Tellier (CEO) and Michael Sabia (CFO); Hunter Harrison (CEO) and Claude Mongeau (CFO); and Claude Mongeau (CEO), Keith Creel (COO); and later Jim Vena (COO),

Luc Jobin (CFO), J.J. Ruest (executive vice-president and chief marketing officer), and Sean Finn (executive vice-president, corporate services, and chief legal officer), have all been attentive to our financial performance and the growth that went with it.

AS THE BOARD of a fully functioning public company, our job was to look to ways to grow the business, and the first item on our list after the IPO was the possibility of acquiring CP's eastern lines. Paul Tellier approached CP, but after waiting months for a response, we decided we were wasting time when NAFTA had made the process of doing business throughout North American much easier.

"Why don't we look across the border?" I said.

Paul agreed and soon the board was hearing about opportunities to build a truly North American railroad. This was a big game-changer for CN, and after considering various options, management zeroed in on Illinois Central. It was well located (Chicago to New Orleans) in relation to our railroad and was very efficiently managed. And it was probably for sale—at the right price. Paul Tellier was enthusiastic and presented me with some preliminary numbers to take to the board. I felt we needed to slow down and analyze the deal more carefully before bringing it to the board. I was concerned because the numbers were too high and I was mindful of the advice from my good friend and Canadian business legend Jimmy Pattison: "When you're looking at buying a company, your due diligence will never show all deficiencies, so always have some *walkabout money.*"

I talked to Paul and said I thought the Illinois Central deal was too expensive and there was no walkabout money. He had no idea what I meant but rather than give a brief tutorial on the wisdom of Jimmy Pattison, I countered with a suggestion that would bridge the gap between Paul's enthusiasm and my caution.

"Instead of presenting the deal to the board," I said, "let's present it to our strategic planning committee. We have some smart, business-savvy people on it. Let's get their reaction first."

Paul agreed, but the reaction from the committee was the same as mine. It was a great idea, but we needed to get it at a better price. Illinois Central was a railroad that had undergone a very fast transition from a big underperformer to having the lowest operating ratio in the industry. To get there, a lot of financial analysis had been done and we were worried that if we paid too much, it might not turn out to be such a great deal. I got a phone call from Paul the next day. He was somewhat annoyed and said that for a bunch of guys who claimed to be entrepreneurs, none of us could see what a great deal this was.

"That's not what we're saying at all," I said. "We think it is the right deal, but it needs fine tuning."

In defense of entrepreneurs, I added that if there was one thing I knew about entrepreneurs it was that they can all see the upside in any deal because it is obvious, but the good ones are a lot more careful about the downside.

"And the reason we're so careful," I continued, "is that most of us risk our own capital and we can't afford to lose it."

With that settled, we agreed to talk again in October 1997, but the deal then was much the same. I was in Europe at the time and we had just had a stock market adjustment, so things in the economy were a little shaky. We agreed to wait for a better price.

JANUARY 1998

Paul was on the phone with the news we had been waiting for.

"The chairman of Illinois Central just left my office," he said.

"What's the price?" I asked.

It was $800 million less that it had been in April.

"Okay," I said, "you have the fish on the line! He's not landed yet, but he's ready to be played and landed."

Paul brought the deal to the board and we gave him the green light to land the fish.

Buying a Class 1 railroad such as Illinois Central required it to pass muster of the Surface Transportation Board (STB) in the U.S., which could take eighteen to twenty-four months. Other railroads could intervene and the STB was concerned with competitive issues. In the meantime, the deal was held in trust pending STB approval—usually with conditions. Illinois Central would continue to run a railroad and CN could not control it. We could put a couple of directors on the board but only for general oversight of management.

One of Illinois Central's great assets was its CEO, Hunter Harrison, so we decided to appoint Hunter executive vice-president and COO of CN immediately and take our chances getting Illinois Central approved at the STB. It was a frustrating process, but with Hunter on board, he could begin to implement operating changes at CN that would make us even more efficient.

Railroads use a measure called operating ratio (OR) to gauge their efficiency. It really means "how many cents does it cost to earn a dollar." When CN was privatized in 1995, our OR was in the high eighties. Today, it is in the low sixties, which is a huge improvement from 1995. Thanks to the work of our management team, this was mostly achieved through responsible cost-cutting and careful revenue growth.

Hunter went to work. He showed us how we could get rid of 20 percent of our locomotives by lengthening our trains. It required some capital to lengthen sidings, but the investment was well worth it. In addition, he introduced the concept of "scheduled railroading". Until then, trains would only move when they were loaded and ready to go. Hunter's idea was to look at the system and work on a schedule. This required some discipline from our customers, but once it was implemented, they could expect better reliability and predictability of service.

He made many other changes. Railroads were notorious for doing things the same way year in and year out. Now there was a fresh set of eyes looking for better ways of doing things. An example was "hump yards." Railroads over the years assembled trains by running them up a little slope, called a "hump," and then using gravity to place the car on the right track. Hunter felt this was an outdated practice and there were more efficient ways to assemble a train.

On May 25, 1999, we received the STB's approval and Illinois Central became part of CN. Our market capitalization increased by about $1 billion. Paul Tellier tackled the STB approval process with vigor. His background in government made him uniquely qualified to work within the system to get most of what we needed in the STB approval process. He had the patience and wisdom to understand the process and he worked hard on it. Many CEOs would have delegated it to others, not wanting to spend a lot of time with bureaucrats, but not Paul. He was well aware of the importance of the decision to us, and he applied all of his experience to ensure we got the right result. He delivered in spades!

WITH ILLINOIS CENTRAL under our belt, we were a true North American railroad. We were no longer totally dependent on transporting western Canada's resources to market (though this would always be an important part of our business), and we had a much bigger pond to swim in. The success of the Illinois Central deal gave us great credibility with the street. We were now a serious player in the business and the efficiency of our operation was the envy of the industry. Paul was energized by this. He had the taste of a big deal and was ready for another one. It wasn't long in coming, but there would be a few lapses in communication along the way.

The most important role of the non-executive chair is to ensure they understand their role in the organization and don't think they are the CEO. It is an art more than a science and to do a really good job takes experience, sensitivity, and good communication skills. Equally important, the non-executive chair has to develop and maintain a good working relationship with the CEO based on respect, good communication, and fairness. It is a tricky combination that can range, on occasion, from defending the CEO to ensuring the CEO remembers they report to the board through the chair. It is a delicate balance for both parties and small wonder if it occasionally tips off-kilter.

In late November 1999, Paul called to tell me CN had structured a deal to take over Burlington Northern Santa Fe.

"We need a board meeting on December 20 to approve the deal," he said.

"Paul," I said, "this is the first time I have ever heard of this deal."

No response.

"Paul, this is a sizeable deal to present to the board on little notice," I said.

Paul replied that it was a huge opportunity and we had to move fast.

We agreed to have a board meeting on December 20, but I forewarned Paul that he might not like the mood of the board. To prepare for the meeting, background papers began to flow to the board and it became clear that if we were to do this "merger," half of our board was expected to resign, including all of our American directors. The new board would consist of eight CN directors and seven Burlington Northern Santa Fe directors. This did not warm the hearts of the board members who were expected to resign.

I called Paul a few days before the meeting to tell him I planned to have the board meet for dinner the night before.

The board had significant concerns about the deal and I felt we should talk about it *en famille* over dinner. He said that he had lawyers, consultants, and bankers to brief and would not be able to attend.

The rest of us met for dinner as planned, and the board members were very concerned. Although they understood that certain potential strategic transactions had to be considered rapidly, they would not be pressured and insisted that they be given sufficient time and information to properly consider the BNSF deal. We met for three hours and at the end of the evening reached a consensus.

We agreed to meet with Paul the next morning. Each board member would have their say, but no bankers, lawyers, or other consultants would be invited to join us until our discussion was over. I called Paul and outlined our plan for the meeting and we all reconvened in the morning.

To his credit, Paul presented the deal exactly the way he saw it. It was a unique opportunity to do a big deal because Robert Krebs, the CEO of Burlington Northern Santa Fe, was about to retire. CN had a prohibition on anyone owning more than 15 percent of our stock, but the lawyers and bankers had found a way around this by using stapled stock. It was complicated, but they said it would work. When Paul finished his presentation, you could have cut the tension with a knife.

"Okay," I said, "we are going to go around the table and hear from each board member."

The discussion went on for two hours. I was then asked for my views and spoke last.

"We must all think of what is best for CN. This deal is huge and will forever change CN. It is complicated and involves merging two distinct cultures. My view is there is no such thing as a merger—usually one company absorbs the other. But we've all had our say, so let's hear from the advisors and we'll have another discussion when they're done."

It was going to be a long day.

In came the advisors, some twenty strong. We heard a legal analysis, a banking analysis, an operational analysis, and a regulatory analysis. We brought in lunch and ate during the presentations. It was now late afternoon and people were beginning to tire. When the presentations came to an end, the consultants, bankers, and lawyers were asked to leave. We were down to the short strokes. I asked Hunter Harrison, our executive vice-president and chief operating officer, to tell us what he thought. Hunter made a very short statement saying he knew the deal had been sprung on the board, but if you looked at it objectively, it was a good deal for CN. The board then voted and they agreed to proceed.

The deal of course went to the STB for approval and a few months later they issued a decree saying they were imposing a two-year moratorium on Class 1 railway mergers while they studied the implications of big mergers. Our deal was dead. It was a way for the U.S. government to kill the takeover of a large U.S. railway by a foreign (Canadian) company.

After a short cooling off period, we decided to look at smaller deals. Smaller would enable us to grow slowly but better, one step at a time, as we had done with Illinois Central, successfully incorporating their company into CN's culture.

With that in mind, we looked at Wisconsin Central. It was a logical piece of the puzzle because it owned the track we ran on between Winnipeg and Chicago, which we paid dearly to use. Why not buy them and extend our line? It made a lot of sense because Wisconsin Central was a very large carrier of forest products, which served the printing industry in its area of operation. It was a perfect fit. It also came with an English and Australian railway, which we spun off. Wisconsin Central was an important link to the U.S. market. We were now the largest carrier of forest products in North America.

Our next deal was Great Lakes Shipping. This was U.S. Steel's shipping system to move their raw product on the Great Lakes. We saw it as a great source of business for the railway, so we did that deal in a heartbeat.

Next up was B.C. Rail, which was suddenly put on the market. The board's assessment was that it was not unlike CN prior to the IPO—a bloated, overstaffed, inefficient Crown corporation. It turned out to be a bidding contest with a preliminary bid followed by a final bid. At first impression, it appeared that B.C. Rail was not worth much, but management analyzed it and found some tax pools we could use to offset other income. We prepared a preliminary bid and after a long board discussion gave Hunter (who was now our CEO) a range of prices up to $1.1 billion to make a final bid. He did and we were the highest bidder. It has turned out well because of our northern B.C. line, which enables us to move products efficiently to the U.S. Midwest.

The last acquisition was a small railroad owned by U.S. Steel that goes around Chicago called the EJ&E (the Elgin,

Joliet and Eastern). The EJ&E was not being very efficiently run by U.S. Steel and we saw an opportunity to circumvent the congestion in Chicago. We put in a bid of $300 million and did the deal. There were a lot of environmental and crossing issues, so it took awhile and some extra investment on our part, but eventually we secured the EJ&E, which made our whole system more efficient. We now had our railway functioning efficiently between three coasts.

16

"There can't be a crisis next week.
My schedule is already full."
HENRY KISSINGER

Crisis Management

ONE OF THE STRONGEST mandates of the CN board is to ensure that CN earns and protects its reputation as a responsible corporate citizen. Some days this is easier than others, but at no time is it more critical than in the aftermath of a situation in which a company's reputation for doing the right thing is put to the test. My father's response to the Canoe River tragedy of 1950 left a deep impression on me of what it means to be a leader in a tough situation. When he got in the car that long ago night, he was instinctively doing the right thing in a crisis: he was showing up. During my years with CN, I have seen many examples of this type of leadership, along with a few missteps that required board intervention. The two that come to mind happened within a few days of each other in the summer of 2005.

Lake Wabamun is a beautiful lake about sixty-five kilo-metres east of Edmonton. You can get there by train and I used to go there as a boy with my friends to swim and fish for pike. It was as close to a summer resort as I could get in those days and I loved it. The name Wabamun comes from the Cree word for "mirror," and on bright summer days, the water is clear and blue. It is not a deep lake or a large one, but it is very popular with people in the surrounding areas and home to cottages and permanent residences that line the shore.

CN was transporting heavy bunker C fuel oil from Edmonton to Vancouver when a twelve-metre section of a replacement rail broke off and forty-three cars of bun-ker C crude oil poured into Lake Wabamun. More than 700,000 litres washed across the surface of the lake. The spill was much smaller than another famous oil spill inci-dent, the Exxon Valdez disaster in Alaska, but because it had occurred in a shallow body of fresh water and because the lake was surrounded by cottages and full-time homes, it was a major crisis for the environment, the people in the area, and CN. And because Lake Wabamun is only forty-five minutes from major newsrooms in Edmonton, the incident generated extremely intense media interest.

CN's management was slow to react. In fairness, this was the first time CN had faced such a situation and it was felt, at least initially, that officers from CN operations who were on the ground were in the best position to do all that was required to address the impact of the accident.

It was obvious to everyone on the board that our

corporate principles demanded we take responsibility and make a commitment to do whatever was necessary to clean up the spill. First, we needed to get a senior executive to the area with the authority to commit the company to act and the right leadership approach to making things happen. Sean Finn, our chief legal officer, was chosen and he did a great job. He visited Lake Wabamun and Edmonton immediately and with his intelligence and respect for the gravity of the situation addressed the concerns of homeowners and government regulators. He also brought in Peter Jones from Vancouver, an expert in crisis management, who assisted in developing a strategy to manage the crisis. After much wrangling and almost a week after the incident, CN took out a full-page ad in the *Edmonton Journal* to present an open letter signed by Hunter Harrison, which said, in effect, that CN would do "whatever it takes for as long as it takes" to clean up Lake Wabamun.

Sean attended numerous meetings to get a handle on the situation and determine a course of action. He met with the lawyer representing the homeowners and established a good rapport and a direct line of communication. Alberta, being a landlocked province, did not have enough oil spill crews equipped to clean up a large body of water, so Sean brought in crews from all over North America, who were charged with undertaking a state-of-the-art cleanup of the affected area. He then travelled several times to London, England, to meet with CN's insurers and personally explain the situation to them in detail. Our insurers reacted very positively to Sean's steady and fulsome flow of information and funded the cleanup, which cost in excess of

$100 million. CN had to pay a $25 million deductible, but the insurers, thanks to the work of Sean Finn, funded the balance without any issues.

The insurance funds enabled Sean, Peter Jones, and others to carry out the board's mandate to leave no trace of the oil spill. As time passed and the homeowners and government regulators saw evidence of the massive cleanup effort, CN was commended for taking responsibility. This was an important turning point in a tough situation and an example of what a company like CN would do to protect its reputation as a responsible company.

Today, after almost eight years of work, Lake Wabamun has returned to its previous state, and the homeowners, though justly critical of CN's early response to the incident, are more complimentary of our follow-through to make things right. In addition to the costly environmental cleanup, CN also invested heavily in communications with homeowners to inform and consult them as we moved forward.

We learned important lessons from the Wabamun spill. First, that a senior executive of the company with full decision-making ability must attend a serious incident to show the company's commitment and authority. Second, that the company must be prepared to act quickly, or it risks letting public opinion spin out of control. Third, that CN must not assume, even in Canada's major oil-producing province, that provincial authorities will be fully equipped for such an incident.

AUGUST 5, 2005 | CHEAKAMUS RIVER CANYON, BC
Two days after the oil spill at Wabamun Lake, nine cars

of a CN-owned B.C. Rail train en route to Vancouver were derailed above the Cheakamus River, spilling a solution of sodium hydroxide into the river that flows into the Squamish River and from there to the sea.

The two rivers are steep and fast-flowing, so the caustic soda moved quickly to the sea. Many fish were killed and there was a huge outcry from the local community, who feared that the rivers where salmon spawned would be dead for a hundred years.

We needed to act quickly to show how concerned we were about these ecologically sensitive spawning rivers. With immediate support from the board, I called Paul Kariya, executive director of the Pacific Salmon Foundation (and uncle of a very well-known local NHL hockey star), and asked him what his five-year budget was to enhance the salmon run in the Cheakamus and Squamish Rivers. He said it was $50,000 a year for five years.

On behalf of CN and with the support of the board, I said we would give him five times that amount—$250,000 a year for five years—to revitalize and rejuvenate all of the rivers affected in the aftermath of the spill. He was most appreciative and I knew the Salmon Foundation would spend every nickel carefully. They had an excellent reputation and we trusted their judgement.

As expected, the Salmon Foundation proceeded to take charge and discovered that although the spill killed many fish, including salmon, it also cleaned out some fish that were not helpful to the salmon run. Within five years, the rivers were in better shape than ever, with even better salmon runs. The *Globe and Mail* followed the story closely and wrote an article about the river's recovery on

August 20, 2010, called "A River Lives Through It." The title was an allusion to the Robert Redford movie *A River Runs Through It,* which, appropriately enough, was about fly-fishing.

"Five years after disastrous B.C. spill," read the article, "the Cheakamus River teems with life." The article commented favourably on CN's actions in addressing the situation quickly and responsibly, which was gratifying, but more importantly, it affirmed our mandate to take full responsibility for our actions no matter what the circumstances. When you make a mistake, you need to own it, you need to fix it, and you need to do whatever it takes to prevent it from happening again.

FEBRUARY 28, 1994 | *VANCOUVER*

It is my father's memorial service and I am giving the eulogy. We are not expecting a big crowd. Dad lived a long life and most of his friends are gone. Few people have the ability to live to ninety-five years of age and enjoy good health to the end, but Dad was fortunate. He was fiercely independent and he died peacefully watching an Olympic hockey game on TV. I can't think of a better way for him to make his final exit, but what can I say that will sum up the life of such a careful and thoughtful man? That he was a good and caring father who provided a stable home environment? That he loved to pay his bills? I remember when he was ninety-three, he decided he would file his own tax return and sent the tax department several thousand dollars just in case he did owe something. It took me months to get it back. I guess the tax department didn't share his sense of integrity.

I decide to begin with the fundamental truth about my father's character and let the stories unfold from there.

"Frank McLean," I say, "was a basic man with basic values. He was a producer in our society—always a giver; never a taker. He had an intense sense of fairness and civic duty, and always believed you should take responsibility for yourself no matter what the circumstances. Responsibility was the foundation of his life and a legacy he leaves to his children and grandchildren—no matter what the circumstances."

17

"Earn your leadership
every day."
MICHAEL JORDAN

Three CEOs

I USED TO THINK that working with a good CEO was akin to working with a thoroughbred racehorse. Jerk the reins too hard or too quickly and the horse will veer off course and may stumble. Pull lightly on the reins and the horse will alter its course and can win the race. Clearly, you don't hire a champion of any stripe and ask them to walk, but I have learned that a healthy and productive relationship between a board chair and the CEO is not about who rides and who runs. It is about mutual respect for complementary strengths and a reliable system of communication. Both parties need to understand this clearly and commit to practising them throughout the tenure of their relationship.

The truth is most CEOs are full of energy and enthusiasm, especially for new deals. But growth for growth's sake is not a good strategy. And growth because a CEO wants to be the "biggest among the bigs" is not a good strategy.

Good strategy is a strong CEO leading a disciplined and accomplished management team, and an equally strong board who looks carefully at acquisitions to see if they are really accretive and will benefit the company in its long-term strategic growth. The CEO may want to push forward and the chair may want to pull back, but who really holds the reins in this equation? The board does—on behalf of the shareholders and on behalf of what the board believes to be in the best interests of the company.

In the past nineteen years, I have had the privilege of working with three outstanding chief executive officers. Each one brought a unique set of skills to the job that benefited CN and its shareholders, and I have learned different things about leadership from all of them.

A STRONG LEADER sets the tone, establishes the goals, and insists that they be met. Paul Tellier did all of these things. He came to CN in 1992 after a remarkable career in the Canadian public service that culminated in his appointment as clerk of the Privy Council, the top civil servant position in Canada.

He became a CEO later than most people and, coming from a government background, he had his detractors. They were soon silenced by his performance. When I rejoined the CN board in August 1994, he had already worked prodigiously to begin preparing CN for privatization. His capacity for hard work was legendary, and by 1994, he had made numerous positive changes at CN by downsizing employees and management. He was committed to doing what needed to be done to get the company ready for the IPO. Under Paul's watch, CN cleaned up its balance sheet by disposing of all non-rail assets. We had $3 billion of debt and very little real equity. We sold off the oil and gas division, the real estate, and various other non-core assets so that by the time of the IPO, our debt was about $1 billion and our equity in excess of $2 billion. Paul was thorough and well organized, and by the fall of 1995, we were ready for the IPO.

My role shifted on the night of the IPO, and we had a discussion about his role as CEO and mine as a non-executive chairman. I made it clear to Paul that I knew my new role would be leading the board, whereas Paul, as CEO, would manage the company and act as its spokesperson. Prior to the IPO, my role had been a little different, because as chairman of a Crown corporation, I was appointed by the shareholder to represent the government of Canada, and needed to be hands-on in approving business decisions affecting that shareholder. Before and after the IPO, we got along well, and I respected his leadership and ensured our board meetings were meaningful, efficient, and focussed on the important issues.

In the late fall of 2002, CN scheduled a meeting of the HR committee in Toronto. We were to meet in Purdy Crawford's boardroom, but I arrived early and was asked to join Purdy and Paul in one of the other conference rooms. Paul surprised us by telling us he was resigning. I was not totally surprised. A man of Paul Tellier's energy and talent is always looking for new challenges. He had done great things at CN, but in the aftermath of the Burlington Northern Santa Fe deal, he may have felt there were not as many mountains to climb at CN.

Purdy and I wished him the best of luck. I said his decision "would change a few things," but I wanted to have the HR committee meeting before we said anything to anyone. We had eight CN directors waiting for us in the boardroom, which was a majority.

"Let's have the meeting," I said, "and when we finish, I'll give you an opportunity to tell the directors what you've just told me. Then I want you to leave so we can have an in-camera discussion."

I told him that in light of his decision I would cancel a trip to Ottawa and instead travel with him to Montreal.

The HR meeting took a couple of hours, and when it came to a close, I told the directors that Paul had an announcement. Paul explained that he was resigning to become CEO of another company but was not yet able to divulge the name of that company. He left the meeting and everyone shifted into transition mode. We had trained for years for just such an event and had a succession plan in place that was reviewed annually by our HR committee. In fact, we had succession plans in place for all of our senior officers that were reviewed in detail each year, usually in the presence of coaches and consultants who had worked with individual executives throughout the year to improve their skills. The CEO was always a key player in these sessions and at the end of them, with only the board present, I would always ask the CEO one final question: "If you got hit by a bus tomorrow, who is your selection to be CEO?"

The board would then hold a discussion at our in-camera session where we would ask a slightly differently worded question: "Who is the best person to lead this company into the future?"

The "best person" had to comply with a set of criteria that included a number of requirements, some of which were more tangible than others.

1. They had to know how to operate the business.
2. They had to be a strategic thinker.
3. They had to understand the importance of succession planning and be prepared to devote considerable time to it among management.
4. They had to understand labour relations and know how to effectively deal with these issues, whether it was unions, compensation matters, or just motivating management.
5. They had to be a leader. In other words, they had to have the "royal jelly." This was somewhat subjective, but you can usually spot a leader when they are faced with a tough situation. Did they display judgement and vision? This was a difficult thing to measure but critical in separating good senior executives from CEOs.

So there we were in the fall of 2002. Paul Tellier had resigned and our job now was to show strong leadership and manage the transition.

"We have to move decisively and quickly to fill the void created by Paul's departure," I said. "He is widely known and respected and he is our 'founding CEO,' so we don't have the luxury of time. A ship doesn't function for long without a captain."

The board affirmed that Hunter Harrison was the logical successor, and I undertook the task of making the necessary phone calls. First on the list was Hunter, but he had already heard about Paul's resignation from Paul, so he wasn't surprised by "the news." Well, he was about to be.

"How would you like to be the new CEO of CN?" I said.

His enthusiasm was palpable. A railroader to his core, he said it was a boyhood dream come true. I told him I was heading to Montreal shortly and we should meet. Hunter said he had a few things planned for the afternoon but would cancel them.

"No need for that," I said. "Finish your day and don't send out any clues that something is up. Keep everything in the strictest confidence. Let's meet tomorrow in Montreal."

The secrecy was necessary because we needed to prepare our public affairs people and legal team to make a coordinated announcement. I also wanted time to meet with our two executive vice-presidents, Jim Foote and Claude Mongeau. And of course, I wanted to talk to the board members who had not been present at the HR meeting.

Paul and I had a relaxed discussion en route to Montreal. It seemed as if a burden had been lifted off his shoulders, and he was clearly energized by the challenges that lay ahead. We discussed the game plan to meet with Claude and Jim and get them onside, and the need for time to prepare the announcement. He agreed to keep it quiet and said he had to coordinate with his new employer to ensure their announcement was made at the appropriate time.

When we got to Montreal, I met with Jim and Claude separately and told them the news of Paul's resignation and of the board's decision to appoint Hunter as the new CEO. They agreed it was the right choice and confirmed their support. A board meeting was set for the following day. It was short notice, but the majority of the board wanted to be present.

We met in the late afternoon and after an hour of in-camera discussion passed a resolution accepting Paul's resignation as of December 31, 2002, and appointing Hunter Harrison as CEO effective January 1, 2003. I asked Hunter to join us. We stood and gave him a rousing standing ovation. A new era had begun at CN.

HUNTER HARRISON WAS very different from Paul Tellier. Paul's Ottawa-honed diplomatic skills were well known and there were few who had not felt the velvet touch of his disarming manner. Hunter had his own approach. First, he was a railroad operator through and through and, second, he was an American with proud roots in Memphis, Tennessee. He was direct in his views and did not suffer fools gladly, but his decisions were always grounded in a focus on efficiency. CN prospered under Hunter's leadership. We completed the B.C. Rail and EJ&E deals, which strengthened our franchise. Our relationship was good and I appreciated his straightforward approach to our respective roles at CN.

"You run the board, David, and I'll run the company," he said.

Hunter had officially joined CN as vice-president and COO in 1998, during our purchase of Illinois Central, but we delayed adding him to the board for almost a year because we wanted to see how well he and Paul worked together. In 1998, Paul requested that Hunter be added to the board, and in December of 1999, Hunter became a director.

At the end of each calendar year, it was my practice to review the performance of each director. I remember a meeting with Hunter that took place in my Montreal office at the end of his first year on the board. He had been missing some board functions. After a brief preamble, I said, "Don't take yourself out of the leadership sweepstakes."

"What did you say?"

"Hunter," I said, "you may be sending signals to the board that you are not really interested in the top job at CN. You should take the opportunity to get to know our directors, so if we had to appoint a new CEO, you would not be taking yourself out of the running.

"I just assumed Paul would be here for years and the top job would not be available," he said.

"Don't make that assumption," I said. "If you're interested in being a serious candidate, you need to engage with the board."

He thanked me and left. A few minutes later, my phone rang. It was Paul Tellier.

"What did you say to Hunter?" he asked me. "He just came down here three feet off the ground."

I told Paul what had transpired, but I don't think either of us anticipated how quickly Hunter's opportunity would arrive. During the next year, however, Hunter engaged far more with the board than he had before, so when we had to make that critical decision about a new CEO, there was no opposition.

Hunter wanted his family to remain in Chicago. We agreed but suggested he get himself a condo in Montreal. He continued to focus on efficiency and we prospered. When the economic events of 2008 struck, CN suffered very little compared with other companies. CN had a proven track record of stable earnings and good cash flow. Under

Hunter's watch, our stock soon recovered to where it had been before the economic crisis.

CN appointed Hunter as its President and CEO effective January 1, 2003. We signed an employment agreement with him on April 22, 2004, which replaced his previous employment agreement and set his terms of employment until December 31, 2008. This was followed by a final and one-year extension to the end of 2009, at which point Hunter would be sixty-five. It was time to look forward. The timing was right for new leadership and the board was clear on its choice. Effective January 1, 2010, Claude Mongeau would be our new CEO. Hunter met with Claude throughout 2009, and they worked closely to ensure a seamless transition.

I always liked Hunter Harrison. He marched to his own drummer, but he was a smart, charming, and very engaging individual who applied his leadership to CN's growth and prosperity.

CLAUDE MONGEAU HAD been with CN for fourteen years when he became CEO. He is an exceptional executive and leader and the prime strategist behind the highly successful rail acquisitions that extended CN's reach throughout North America and made it a key industry player. In appointing Claude, the board was confident he would continue to build on CN's previous successes but renew management's attention to the concerns and issues facing our customers and stakeholders.

From the moment he was appointed CEO, Claude Mongeau set out to strengthen the confidence of our customers and stakeholders. He travelled extensively and met one-on-one with key executives who represented our customers and our stakeholders. Claude is a good listener and, as a result of his consultations, was able to work quickly and effectively in making the necessary changes. It became clear to the board that within a short time he had accomplished a great deal to improve confidence in CN.

Claude is a visionary leader. He leads by example and has put together a strong leadership team with plenty of depth. When Keith Creel, CN's executive vice-president of operations, left to become president of CP, Claude replaced him with Jim Vena, a seasoned and smart CN executive who had been running CN in the U.S. There was never a vacuum in leadership. Jim transitioned smoothly at a time when leadership in this important executive role was strongly needed.

The board is well briefed by Claude's team on all strategic issues. The board's strategic planning committee, which is led ably by Hugh Bolton, provides in-depth background that makes for informed and lively board discussions. Claude is a great team leader, allowing each of his key executives to present their views. Board feedback is positive and useful, and there is much to be gained by all sides in such a well-prepared environment for discussion.

I have great respect for Claude's leadership and the high standards he sets for himself. Each year, we review Claude's performance, and he always understates where he ranks. Claude Mongeau leads by example and it shows. He has grown a great deal as CEO, fully justifying the confidence the board placed in him when he was selected.

EACH OF THE three CEOs I have worked with at CN brought energy and vision to their leadership. All of them are gifted, have strengths and weaknesses, and have left their leader-ship stamp on the organization. Hunter Harrison always said that if you focus 90 percent of the CEO's time on devel-oping your people, the rest will follow. I agree. People are at the heart of our business, and we must be able to stand their comings and goings and manage transitions smoothly. It is the board's duty and responsibility to ensure that this applies as much to them as it does to everyone else.

18

"If you don't know where
you're going, you'll end up
someplace else."
YOGI BERRA

The Future

IT MAY STRIKE the wrong chord to begin a discussion about
the future of CN with a nod to the past, but during its long
life as a Crown corporation, I often felt that CN was viewed
with a certain degree of contempt by its main rival, CP. In
some ways this was justified.

CN was like a kid with a rich father who can spend freely
on whatever is wanted at the time without much account-
ability. The deep pockets of the Canadian government, and
by extension the many pockets of Canadian taxpayers,
enabled CN to spend more freely on capital improvements
and the maintenance of their rail system than they would
have been able to under different circumstances. It earned
CN various monikers over the decades, which included
being named Canada's "gold-plated railway."

I admit that CN's spending as a Crown corporation
was unsustainable, but included in that spending was a

gold-plated commitment to safety. I make no apology for that commitment, which continues to this day. Safety is critical to the operation of a railway. I learned that long before I became chairman of the board. I learned that the day my father got in the car and drove to Canoe River.

Ironically, it was overspending (in the right areas) that made CN such an ideal candidate for privatization because there were no deferred maintenance issues. The public was the beneficiary of a very good rail system on November 28, 1995, but it is what we did with that system after the IPO that is the real story. Motivated and supported by the board, CN's management proceeded to build one of the greatest freight railways in the world. Year after year, CN has created solid shareholder value, because our business model is grounded in what we call our climate of excellence. It is not particularly remarkable that we created it. What is remarkable is that we have sustained it year in and year out for the past nineteen and a half years.

CP, however, never went through the fundamental changes we did in preparation for the IPO or in the years that followed—and in 2011, we began to hear rumblings that Hunter Harrison was planning to come out of retirement and run CP! The play for CP was orchestrated by Pershing Square Capital Management and its founder and CEO, William (Bill) Ackman. CP was clearly in need of a railroader, so they approached Hunter, who became their CEO after their annual meeting in the spring of 2012. It resulted in a major restructuring of CP's board of directors.

At CP, Hunter cut costs, announcing that 4,500 employees would be let go in an attempt to restructure the company.

He applied his "Hunter principles of railroading" to CP. He lengthened trains, eliminated unnecessary overhead, and eliminated the need for equipment (including locomotives)—all of which generally made CP much more efficient. CP stock improved in a relatively short period of time and shareholders, after many years of poor stock performance, saw the value of their shares more than double. Hunter did what we all knew needed to be done. CP had to be re-engineered to become a more efficient and focussed operation. But I guess it took a CN man to do it.

Early in 2013, Hunter recruited one of CN's up and coming senior executives, Keith Creel, to serve as CP's president and chief operating officer. Keith was clearly being groomed as a successor to Hunter. Again, it was what needed to be done, and I give CP full credit for having the courage and determination to do it. I have the highest regard for Keith Creel, who left CN on the best of terms. Keith is not only one of the finest railroad operators in North America, he is a gentleman with a wonderful sense of values. He will do well at CP, but on the home front, CN took steps to protect the rest of its senior management team from "recruitment" through to the end of 2016.

There are many challenges ahead for CP. Cost-cutting is only the first step in establishing a successful railroad, but in the long run, the improvements at CP will benefit CN. We can cooperate with CP to take advantage of mutual synergies, and there's nothing like a little home-based competition to keep the mind focussed.

Only time will tell where CP goes in the future, but CN will not be standing around watching. CN is an exceptionally strong, well-capitalized company and very well equipped to sell its own newspapers long into the future. That future will include a board of directors and a new chairman whose commitment to acting in the best interest of the company will remain at the forefront of their decisions.

AUGUST 2013 | *VANCOUVER*

I am sitting in my den at my home in Vancouver working on my memoir. I like to write in longhand and have amassed a great stack of notes, which an assistant deciphers and types up and then delivers to my writing partner, Tricia Finn. She flinches when she sees me coming. How much more is he going to write? I hear her thinking. Together, we keep the book moving forward, so I try not to agitate her too much. My biggest challenge is keeping the manuscript away from Brenda. Brenda is an editorial slasher. She can take ten pages I have slaved over and reduce them to one. I am beginning to suspect she finds my life story tiresome.

"Gaga."

"Gaga is very busy right now, Liam. Where's Gamma?"

My grandson is three years old and like his sister, Hazel, one of the very few people in the world who get to call me Gaga to my face. Liam's head comes to the top of my desk. His hair rises above it and I don't always hear him come in.

"Can I play with your trains?

My trains are models and are displayed on shelves above Liam's reach in my den. I explain to Liam that my trains are not toys. They are gifts from organizations I have spoken to about CN, presented to me, chairman of the board, and they are special. I am about to mention my nineteen and a half years of service, but Liam interrupts me.

"Are you playing with the trains, Gaga?"

"Gaga is writing a book."

"You could get the trains down."

I put down my pen. A teaching moment. My wonderful little grandson will benefit from a brief lecture about leadership. I decide to take a break from writing and share my wisdom with a three-year-old.

"Liam," I say, "the mark of a good leader is the ability to listen, respect the views of others, and take full responsibility for their actions, as CN did after an oil spill at Wabamun Lake. The last time I let you play with my trains, you left them in Henry's bed. I am willing to share my trains with you, but I need to know you will treat them with respect and return them to my den and not leave them in Henry's bed now or in the future."

"Can I play with the remote?"

"What's on your hands? Did Gamma give you a sticky bun?"

"Yes."

"Are there any left? Liam?"

But he's already gone. Head down, I return to my manuscript and a few closing remarks about corporate governance.

THE ROLE OF the chair is to lead the board in the selection and motivation of a good CEO, to lead the board to perform at a high level, and to always act in the best interest of the company. We successfully rebuilt the board in preparation for the IPO, but directors—like CEOs—come and go. Part of my job as chairman over the years has been to anticipate and prepare for changes while continuing to raise the bar. Here are a few examples of some of the changes to the board of directors we have made over the years and the strategy that drove them.

In the spring of 1996, it became apparent that the CN board of directors would benefit from some American directors. We were seeking ways to increase our revenue stream and looking at U.S. acquisitions.

Our first choice was Michael Armellino, BS, MBA, CFA, a retired partner in Goldman Sachs Group and chair and CEO of Goldman Sachs Asset Management from 1991 to 1994. Michael had been the top rail analyst in the United States and was very knowledgeable about the rail industry. It would be difficult to find a better candidate for our board, but our custom was (and is) to wait until the president and chairman met with the candidate separately. This was to ensure the candidate would bring the proper "chemistry" to the board.

In May of 1996, Paul Tellier met with Michael in New York and, a few days later, I met with him in Vancouver. Michael's reputation and accomplishments spoke for themselves, but I was instantly impressed with his basic qualities. He was experienced, committed to CN's continued success, and had excellent business judgement. He has now been on the board for more than seventeen years. He is a trustee and member of the executive committee of the

Peddie School, a trustee of the Hackensack University Medical Center Foundation, and founder and senior advisor of the Bergen Volunteer Medical Initiative, a privately funded organization that provides free health care to those without health care in Bergen County, New Jersey.

With Michael officially on board on May 7, 1996, we decided it would be wise to have two more American directors, preferably one with Democratic connections and one with Republican connections.

Gordon D. Giffin was U.S. ambassador to Canada under President Bill Clinton from 1997 to 2001. He was, in the opinion of many Canadians, the best ambassador the U.S. ever sent to Canada. I was always struck by Gordon's great insight into Canadian issues. This stemmed, in part, from his background. Born in Massachusetts, Gordon had been raised in Montreal and Toronto and attended schools in Pointe-Claire and Etobicoke. An attorney by profession, Gordon had a BA from Duke University and a JD from Emory University School of Law in Atlanta. Gordon later became a member of a number of important corporate boards, including Canadian Imperial Bank of Commerce, Canadian Natural Resources, TransAlta Corporation, and Ontario Energy Savings Corp. Gordon Giffin really understood our country and our industry. He joined our board on May 1, 2001, and has made a significant contribution, especially in terms of providing us with valuable insights into U.S. politics.

Our next American director was Edith Holiday, BS, JD, who joined us a month after Gordon, on June 1, 2001. Edith had worked as chief counsel and national financial and operations director for the George H.W. Bush presidential campaign from 1985 to 1988. This was followed by an appointment as assistant to the president of the United States and secretary of the Cabinet in 1990. In the interim, she was general counsel to the U.S. Department of the Treasury. After she left the White House, she served as a director on many important corporate boards, including H.J. Heinz, Hess Corporation, RTI International Metals, and White Mountains Insurance Group, and she is a trustee and director of various investment companies of the Franklin Templeton Group of Mutual Funds. In 2009, she received the Sandra Day O'Connor Board Excellence Award. This is an award that honours women who have served with distinction on the board of a public company and in doing so advanced "diversity in the workplace." Edith Holiday's experience has been of enormous assistance to CN as we have grown in the U.S.

We also added a number of new Canadian directors to replace some of the original directors who moved on after the IPO. Two of those directors would join us on the same day. In 1996, a decision was made to expand the board to include a director from Alberta. After reviewing a long list of high-profile contenders, the corporate governance committee unanimously recommended Jim Gray.

James K. Gray, OC, AOE, LLD, was a very creative entrepreneur in the oil industry. He co-founded Canadian Hunter Exploration Ltd. in 1973, which became one of Canada's largest and most successful natural gas companies. The company's financial success was matched by its reputation for the care Jim took to foster and create an employee-friendly work culture with an awareness of environmental conservation and stability. Jim was also known for his strong support of community associations, such as the YMCA's summer camps and free swimming programs. This was a reflection of Jim's strong belief that healthy communities and families are the foundation of good business ethics. Jim was an experienced director of numerous companies including Brascan Corporation (now Brookfield Asset Management), Emera, Phoenix Technology Services, and Twin Mining Corporation. When Jim joined the CN board in 1996, he was already an Officer of the Order of Canada and the recipient of an honorary doctorate of laws degree from the University of Calgary and a Citation for Citizenship from the government of Canada. He would be recognized with an Alberta Order of Excellence in 2002 and inducted into the Canadian Business Hall of Fame in 2005. Jim Gray brought tremendous knowledge of the oil and gas industry to the CN board, and when he retired in 2009, he would be unanimously elected director emeritus.

The Hon. Edward C. Lumley, PC, LLD, also joined us on July 4, 1996. Ed had been vice-chairman of BMO Capital Markets (and its predecessor companies) since 1991 and had served as chair of Noranda Inc. from 1986 until 1991. He had also achieved great success in political life, serving as mayor of Cornwall, Ontario, followed by ten years as a Member of Parliament under Prime Minister Trudeau. Ed held a diverse range of senior portfolios in the Trudeau government, which included industry, international trade, regional economic development, communications, and science and technology. He was an outstanding economic development minister. During that time, he also held responsibility for numerous Crown corporations, such as the CBC, the Canada Development Investment Corporation, and Teleglobe (now VSNL International Canada). His commitment to business and public service has been matched by his commitment to education and, in 2006, he was appointed chancellor of his alma mater, the University of Windsor. Ed Lumley's background in government and business has been of great value to CN, both during its transition from Crown corporation to investor-owned company and in the years since. Ed has served on numerous public company boards, including BCE, Air Canada, Magna International, and Dollar Thrifty Automotive Group. Like me, Ed Lumley was a student athlete and, unlike me, the star quarterback of the Junior Windsor AKO Fratmen football team, the year they won an Ontario Championship.

But back to the CN board.

In 2003, we realized we would need a financial expert to satisfy all of the new regulatory rules coming out of the post-ENRON era. To fill that role, we went with Hugh Bolton.

Hugh Bolton, FCA, was the retired chairman and chief executive partner of Coopers & Lybrand, a large accounting firm that had merged with Price Waterhouse. Hugh had been a big part of the merger to create what would be renamed, PricewaterhouseCoopers. At the time of his recruitment to CN, he was chair of Matrikon Inc. and a director of Teck Resources and TD Bank Financial Group. Hugh had moved back to his home in Edmonton after many years in Toronto. We knew he would make a good director, bringing an Alberta point of view to our board. Hugh joined us on April 15, 2003, and brought financial depth few could match. His subsequent board appointments would include Capital Power Corporation and WestJet. He was inducted as a fellow of the Institute of Corporate Directors of Canada in 2006 and, in 2010, honoured with a Lifetime Achievement Award from the Institute of Chartered Accountants of Alberta.

Another one of CN's 2003 appointments was A. Charles Baillie, OC, LLD. CN needed a banker to replace Cedric Ritchie, who was retiring (and is now director emeritus). Ced left big shoes to fill. At the time of his appointment to CN, Charles Baillie was nearing the end of a five-decade career with the Toronto-Dominion Bank. Born in Ontario, he had joined the bank in 1964 after doing an MBA at Harvard Business School. In 1997, he was appointed chairman and chief executive officer of TD Bank, retiring as CEO in 2002 and chairman in 2003. He has served on numerous public company boards, including George Weston Ltd. and Telus, and is chair of the Alberta Investment Management Corporation (AIMCO). Charlie's success in the world of banking has been matched by a commitment to arts and education. He is chancellor emeritus of Queen's University (after six years as chancellor), honorary chair of the Art Gallery of Ontario, and president of Authors at Harbourfront Centre. He also serves on the national board of directors of the Royal Conservatory of Music and Luminato, and on the advisory board of Canada's National History Society. He was appointed an Officer of the Order of Canada in 2006 and inducted into the Canadian Business Hall of Fame in 2008. Charles Baillie's wisdom, good judgement, and unique blend of experience brought new perspective to our board.

In 2011, we added two former CEOs to replace retiring directors Purdy Crawford, Jim Gray, and Raymond Cyr.

Donald J. Carty, OC, LLD, joined us on January 1, 2011. Don is a business leader with a career in the aviation business spanning thirty years. He retired as chairman and CEO of AMR Corporation and American Airlines in 2003, but prior to that, he was president and executive vice-president of finance and planning of AMR Corporation and American Airlines, and president and CEO of Canadian Pacific Air Lines from 1985 to 1987. He was also vice-chair and CFO of Dell Inc. from 2007 to 2008. In the volunteer sector, he is on the executive board of Southern Methodist University's Cox School of Business, is former chairman of Big Brothers Big Sisters of America, and is a former trustee of Queen's University, from which he received an honorary doctorate of laws. Don's board experience is extensive and he is lead director of Barrick Gold Corporation and a director of Talisman Energy Inc. He is chairman of Virgin American Inc. and Porter Airlines. His past directorships include Hawaiian Airlines, Sears, Placer Dome, CHC Helicopter, Dell Inc., and Gluskin Sheff + Associates Inc. Don Carty's impressive experience as a CEO of a major company and corporate director on so many major boards is of great value to CN. Widely recognized on both sides of the border, Don was listed as one of *Board Alert*'s outstanding directors in 1999 and, in 2003, he was named an Officer of the Order of Canada.

James (Jim) O'Connor joined the CN board on April 27, 2011. Jim is the retired chairman and CEO (1998–2011) of Republic Services Inc., a leading provider of non-hazardous solid waste collection, recycling and disposal services in the United States. Prior to 1998, he held management positions at Waste Management Inc. In 2001, Jim was the recipient of the Ellis Island Medal of Honor from the National Ethnic Coalition of Organizations, which awards Americans who exemplify outstanding qualities in their personal and professional lives while continuing to preserve the richness of their particular heritage. He has also been named on the list of America's best CEOs each year between 2005 and 2010, and in 2011, Jim was named to *Institutional Investor*'s All-American Executive Team. Jim's community interests focus on causes that benefit children and he has served on the board of directors of SOS Children's Villages. In keeping with his career path and experience, he currently serves on the board of directors of the Clean Energy Fuels Corp. Jim O'Connor's expertise in waste management, environmental awareness, and strategic planning are of great value to CN, and he will play an important role on the board in the future.

WE HAVE FIVE directors retiring in 2014 and 2015 and the board has worked diligently to fill these positions with directors who will bring strengths to the areas our five departing directors represented in abundance. We have also established the designation of "director emeritus" to honour retired directors who have served a minimum of ten years and made an outstanding contribution to the CN board. Our first four, Purdy Crawford, Raymond Cyr, Jim Gray, and Cedric Ritchie, all gave generously of their time and wisdom and are invited to join us at our annual meeting and at an out-of-town board meeting event we usually hold in the fall. The relationships between our directors emeritus and the current board and management are a reflection of the loyalty, friendship, and respect we feel for one another.

The board will have a new look when I retire, but we are delighted with the choices we have made. The company's needs going forward and our "evergreen" list of potential directors have been carefully researched. Our final choices are an example to others of good director recruitment.

Last is the matter of a new chair.

This issue was brought to the board a few years before I reached the magic age at which all CN directors must step down, to ensure they had time to carefully consider potential candidates. It was decided we had ample leadership talent on the board. As part of the process, I stepped down as chair of the corporate governance committee in 2012 and the board appointed Michael Armellino to succeed me as committee chair. It would be Michael's job to preside over the selection of CN's next chair.

After consulting all board members, and after careful deliberation, the board unanimously chose Robert Pace from Halifax as CN's next chair. It was a great choice. I leave knowing CN's board leadership is in good hands. In addition to his exemplary record as a director, Robert has provided leadership to the board as chair of the audit committee and HR committee for long periods of time and during some difficult economic conditions.

The CN board has been rich in talent since the night of the IPO, and many of us have worked with three different CEOs. We have chosen carefully each time and it has paid huge dividends. We have been successful because of careful board recruitment and the care we have taken in choosing committee leaders. We communicate well with one another and give thoughtful and thorough consideration to all of the important issues facing the company. We have great respect for one another's experience and judgement, and as Michael Armellino once said, "We can disagree without being disagreeable." We all have the best interests of the company at heart and measure ourselves on how well the business is performing. We have good chemistry and I realize more now on the eve of my departure that the good chemistry we created was not just the essence of a good board of directors, it was the reward.

"GAGA."

I am on the home stretch, so I don't respond. I am composing a list of ten things my readers need to know about chairing a board. This is, after all, a business memoir about leadership, not some rambling diatribe about trains and relationships.

The Role of the Chair: Ten Necessary Skills
1. The ability to chair a meeting.
2. The ability to enable a group to reach a consensus decision.
3. The ability to ensure everyone is heard but no one dominates the discussion.
4. The ability to advance a meeting to deal with issues in a timely manner.
5. The ability to sense a crisis and deal with it effectively and quickly.

6. The ability to deliver messages that need to be delivered even if they are a bit painful.
7. The ability to not waste time and ensure the group experience is meaningful and enjoyable.
8. The ability to be tough but fair.
9. The ability to bring discussion to a meaningful conclusion.

"Gaga."

"I'm not finished, Liam," I say, but I look up.

He has his sister with him. Hazel is five and has a year of kindergarten under her belt. They look at me and I look at them. Dead silence. Nobody moves. And then I blink.

I get up from my desk and take the trains down and they leave with my beautiful trains clutched in their sticky little hands. I have one last item to add to my list.

10. The ability to know when your time is up and plan for the future.

PART FOUR

Love and Other Wonders

19

Miracles

AS I WRITE THESE WORDS, Brenda and I have been married for forty-two years. We have followed our dreams and achieved far more together than either of us could ever have imagined doing separately or—God forbid—with anyone else. It has been a wonderful life. Of course, there have been bumps along the way, but we have an incredible connection that has seen us through any storm clouds that have gathered. And gathered they have.

As a driven achiever, I was rarely at peace with myself until I was faced with a life-threatening health crisis. In my case, however, one brush with mortality was not enough. It would take two trips through the lion's den to get the message across and the lessons learned. Was it a miracle that I survived? I don't have the answer to that question, and I am not sure it is really the point. The miracle was not living through a near-miss with acute angina followed by prostate cancer a year later. These conditions are no longer death sentences and with good medical care many people survive them. The miracle was the lesson I learned in the process. The miracle was learning how to pray—not ask, negotiate, purchase, lease, plea bargain, or demand—just find a quiet place inside my own head and pray.

It was 1996 and a year after the IPO. I was busy with my local real estate projects and, in particular, the development of the parcel of city land that would become Vancouver Film Studios. CN stock was on the rise and the post-IPO board of directors was very strong and running smoothly. The intense travel schedule of 1995 (thirty-five trips to Montreal, Ottawa, Toronto, and New York) had lessened to a degree, but travel takes a toll on your health long after the bags are unpacked and you have settled into the right time zone. It is easy to rationalize the aches and pains of a hectic schedule as a temporary sacrifice for whatever cause you are currently chasing.

One day as Brenda and I were returning from our morning walk, I felt a pain in my chest. It was not really a sharp pain but clearly a pain of some sort that intensified as I walked up a slight incline. When I arrived home, the pain went away, so I decided it was just a case of indigestion or a muscle spasm or anything else I could think of that might explain an unfamiliar pain in the middle of my chest without mentioning the obvious.

The next day, the experience repeated and when we got home Brenda called our son Sacha, who was in his last year at Queen's. She described my symptoms to him and his response was the immediate reaction of a son who is brighter than his parents: "Get him to a doctor now. Take him to the hospital. He may have heart issues."

We drove straight to Vancouver General Hospital, where we were met by a young cardiologist who suggested I take a treadmill stress test. No problem. I jumped on the treadmill and started walking, but within seconds, my blood pressure surged and the cardiologist ordered me to stop. He told me I had a blockage and would need an angiogram.

"I'll give you some medication," he said, "and book you in for an angiogram next week."

"All right," I said, "but I have to be in Montreal next Monday and Tuesday for an important CN board meeting. Can I go?"

"Yes," he said, "so long as you take the medication."

He was a young and very well-educated cardiologist, but this turned out to be very bad advice. In fairness to him, I was looking for easy answers, too.

A few days later, I was packing for my trip to Montreal when I had the mother of all chest pains. I called for Brenda who was in another room. I was about to miss my first and only CN board meeting in my nineteen and a half years as chair.

"What is it?" she said.

"You'd better get me to the hospital."

It was eight o'clock on Sunday morning. She phoned the young cardiologist, who met us at the emergency ward at Vancouver General Hospital. He looked very concerned, which alarmed me almost as much as the pain in my chest.

They put me on a bed and sprayed nitroglycerin under my tongue. The young cardiologist said his associate Dr. Ian Penn had just arrived and would be looking in on me shortly. How lucky I was to meet Ian Penn. He saved my life. It was a routine event for him, given his line of work and reputation, but a very big deal for me and my family.

My lower left-descending artery—the one they called the "widow-maker"—was 95 percent blocked. If it had been completely blocked, I would have died that morning before anyone could help me. If I had gotten on the plane, if I had been alone or driving...there were a lot of ifs.

When Ian first came to see me, he touched my arm and I felt my whole body relax. Ian is both a doctor and a healer. He has a spiritual calm about him that gives you confidence and helps ground you. He said that since it was Sunday, he could call in his catheter lab team if he had two patients that needed immediate help. I qualified for immediate help, as did another patient on the ward. In my case, they would do an angiogram, he said, and if necessary an angioplasty, which would involve putting a balloon up an artery from my groin and inflating it so that the blood would flow, and then inserting a stent to keep the artery open.

The latter procedure proved necessary and resulted in a fourteen-millimetre stent being inserted in my artery. I remained in the hospital for several days for observation, and it was lucky I did, because a day or so after the procedure, I tried to stand up and fainted. They discovered I had a false aneurism in my artery at the groin where they had gone in with the stent. So it was back to the operating room for arterial surgery the next day, and a few days later, I was released and sent home.

While I was in the hospital, I did a lot of thinking about the fragility of life and in particular my own. I decided that if I survived this experience, I would get serious about changing my life. I would lose weight and be more responsible about my eating habits. I had never been a drinking man, but there would be no more midnight encounters with the ice cream bucket after a sedentary evening of television sports. I would concede that gravy was not a food group and I would give it up. I would slow down and smell the roses—as literally as possible. I would think about my rose garden in the winter, when the branches were bare, and in August, when they bloomed in abundance, I would share them with others. I wouldn't just go for a morning walk with my wife and my dog because it was good for Henry and because Brenda said it was a nice day and we should go for a walk. I would do it because it was wonderful to be with them and it made me happy to be outside no matter what the weather. And I would not, under any circumstances, go to the office until I had meditated. I was not entirely sure how to meditate, but with Brenda's help, I was going to figure it out.

After a few weeks at home, I went back to the hospital for a follow-up appointment with the young cardiologist. He gave me the all-clear.

"You're okay," he said. "You can go back to work."

"You must be kidding," I said. "I've just had a life-threatening, life-altering experience and you're telling me to go back to work!"

I told him it would be several months before I would return to the office. In the meantime, I was going to change my life and meditate! Calmly! He gave me a look like I had just told him my astrological sign. He had seen my type before. The scientist meets the wing nut. Well, there's nothing like the determination of a wing nut.

I decided to form a spiritual group made up of men I knew and liked in the Vancouver business community. The criteria were simple. They had to be business leaders who were interested in changing their lives and they had to believe (or want to believe) in something bigger than themselves. We had all served on the board of *this* or the board of *that*, but ours would be a spiritual board whose mandate was the health and spiritual well-being of one another. We were not looking for preachers who had all the answers. We decided we would meet every few months over lunch and discuss how we were doing and ask for guidance in prayer, though I think if one of us had dropped to our knees and prayed in a public restaurant, the others would be out the door.

And then I got cancer.

IN 1997, WHEN I was fifty-nine and Brenda was fifty-one, I was diagnosed with prostate cancer. It was serious. The Gleason score, which some readers will be sadly familiar with, is a score between one and ten assigned to prostate cancers to measure their severity. A low score is preferable to a high one. I got a seven and then I got an eight. For the first time in a long time, I wished I had failed an exam, and in a way I had.

I was devastated. My perfect world had been turned upside down a second time in two years and there were no bankers to blame or stents to fix the problem. I was shocked and anxious and very, very sad. "Cancer" is a word we associate with forces beyond our control. Cancer was malignant and insidious. People with cancer fought "battles," and so very many good people "lost" those battles. A heart problem sends you into action. Cancer stops you in your tracks—or so I thought.

I had excellent medical advisors who recommended the removal of my prostate. I decided to give myself a bit of time, so I asked Brenda and the boys to go with me to Ireland, my spiritual home. I needed time to think and ask for guidance—a pilgrimage.

It was a strangely happy trip in many ways, because I was with the three people I loved most. There were no deals to make and no time to waste worrying about them. There was just my beautiful wife and our two blue-eyed sons. Jason was twenty-four and Sacha was twenty-two. Fatherhood had come late to me and I wanted it to last another hundred years.

Our first night in Ireland, we stayed at a lovely old castle called Adare Manor. After dinner, Brenda and I went back to our room and I knelt beside the bed to pray. I could never have done such a thing as a younger man. My previous experiences with organized religion had been uncomfortable and at times oppressive. The assertion of opinion about who was saved and who was not had always been a problem for me and I did not believe in it. But Brenda had quietly changed all that. She had shown me how to open up to a spiritual life without letting the dogma that so often went with it block my path. No one, she said, has an inside track. You have to listen to yourself. Plumb the depths and the answers will come.

That night, I plumbed the depths and listened to myself and when the answer came, it came in the form of a very loud voice inside my head: GO AND LOOK IN YOUR BRIEFCASE.

Can't a man pray in peace? I'm plumbing the depths here, I wanted to say, but the voice in my head was insistent, so I got up off my knees and went over to the desk where I had left my briefcase.

"What are you doing?" Brenda asked.

"I'm looking in my briefcase."

"I thought you were praying," she said.

"I am."

I think if I had pulled out a bank statement, deal memo, or contract at that point, Brenda would have been quite justified in throwing the briefcase and all of its contents out the window, but I did not do any of those things. Instead, she watched quietly as I opened up the briefcase and pulled out an article my brother-in-law had handed me when I left the office.

"You might be interested in this," he said, but I was running late, so I just put it into my briefcase with my other papers and forgot about it.

The article I retrieved now was the story of two men with prostate cancer who had been helped by Chinese medicine. One of them was a man named McLean. I knew this was not a coincidence. I read the article, as did Brenda, and in the morning, I called my doctor in Vancouver and began reading the article out loud to him. He interrupted me—but not to tell me I was a new-age idiot and should quit talking herbs and get back to Vancouver and have my prostate removed.

"I know the guy called McLean," he said.

"Do you have his phone number handy?" I asked.

He did.

The next day, we left Adare Manor and moved to Sheen Falls Lodge in County Kerry. I waited until nightfall and then called the other Mr. McLean. He picked up the phone.

"You don't know me," I said, "but I'm calling you from Ireland to talk about my prostate."

To my surprise, he didn't hang up. Instead, he listened and asked me what the problem was. I told him I had been diagnosed with prostate cancer and was travelling with my family in Ireland. I had found his name on a report about the successful use of Chinese herbs as a treatment for prostate cancer. Yes, he said, it was true. He had used the herbs and his tests had gone from positive to negative.

The discussion that followed went something like this:

He said that although the herbs were important, he believed that his strong spiritual faith was also a big factor in his recovery. I said that I, too, had a strong spiritual belief system (which was getting stronger by the hour). He then mentioned in passing that he had gone to hear Charles Colson speak at the Vancouver Club a week earlier.

Colson was special counsel to Richard Nixon and one of the Watergate masterminds. He was a tough guy who once said he would run over his grandmother if it got Nixon a second term. The press called him a "hatchet man" and an "evil genius." But seven months in an Alabama prison turned his life around, and when he got out of jail he founded a non-profit ministry called Prison Fellowship. Apparently, someone gave him a copy of *Mere Christianity* by C.S. Lewis when he was in jail and he decided the message was the one he had been waiting for.

"You heard Chuck Colson speak at the Vancouver Club?" I said. "I was there, too. What do you look like?"

"I have white hair and a big white beard."

"I remember you well. I was looking at you the whole time, thinking who's the guy with the white hair and white beard sitting across from me? You were under a beam of light from a small window behind your head. It made you look like you had a halo of light around your head. It reminded me of what I thought God looked like when I was a little kid."

He assured me that he was not God, but he did know where I could get the Chinese herbs. I wrote down the details and when I arrived home from Ireland, I went to the herbalist and bought a supply. They needed to be boiled and I was told to drink the mixture as soon as it had cooled slightly. It smelled very strong, but I downed it exactly as instructed, telling myself it would heal me.

I arranged to meet the other Mr. McLean in my office a few weeks after my return to Vancouver. He was a kind and very charming man, a reformed alcoholic, and a staunch member of Alcoholics Anonymous. Clearly, his spiritual side was important to him for reasons other than the one we shared. We decided to say a prayer and, to my surprise, I was not self-conscious.

My next set of tests showed a big improvement over the previous ones. My doctor was surprised and even more surprised when I told him what I had been doing. Encouraged by my results, I said that I did not want to have my prostate removed. I wanted to continue to treat myself using alternative methods. The doctor, who was and is a very prominent prostate cancer specialist and has since become a good friend of mine, kept his thoughts to himself and decided to humour me. That would be fine, he said, so long as I agreed to a have a biopsy every six months.

"I'd like to monitor your progress," he said.

"Absolutely," I said. "Every six months."

My prostate and I left the office and continued with our various treatments, which included Chinese herbs, meditation, prayer, diet, and exercise. I was discovering something important about cancer. It was not a lonely journey. It was a pilgrimage of people from very different backgrounds who were learning how to listen.

One day, I ran into an old friend from Edmonton whose wife had been ill with cancer. They had heard about a salt in Arizona that seemed to help her. It was found in an area of an Indian reserve where the people had a miniscule incidence of cancer. The salt was in their water supply, so everyone in the area was getting it naturally.

"She's doing well," my Edmonton friend said. "It's helping."

I bought some of the Arizona salt pills and spoke to a healer, who told me to take high doses of calcium, magnesium, and Vitamin D with the salt.

"Do this for a month," he said, and I followed his instructions religiously.

I had my next biopsy shortly after this heavy dose of supplements. As usual, I had to wait a few days for the results. I remember coming home from work and driving into our garage. I was on the phone. Brenda was waiting for me with tears in her eyes.

"David, hang up the phone," she said.

I got out of the car and she told me the biopsy was clear and there was no cancer. All of my previous biopsies had shown an improvement but never without a residual number of low-grade cancer cells. But this test was the best I had ever had. It was a perfect score! None of the needles found any signs of cancer. It had taken eighteen months, but a huge weight had lifted from my shoulders. I was a new man and, I think, a better one.

My reprieve lasted eleven years, ending with a trip to the Mayo Clinic in 2008 for a medical checkup. My prostate-specific antigen, or PSA, test showed a reading of twenty-six, which was too high. I called my doctor in Vancouver, who ordered a second PSA test for when I got back. The reading was now forty. How much can you ask? I had been given eleven extra years already. I decided that I was ready for surgery, but the doctor said he wouldn't have to operate. He would treat me with forty external beam radiation treatments. I agreed, and when my forty days and forty nights were over, my PSA levels were under control. It is now 2013, my PSA number is steady at .09, and I feel great.

It has been eighteen years since I came home from the hospital with a stent in my artery and a commitment to plumb the depths. The group of men I asked to join me for spiritual support in 1996 is still together. There are eight of us, and when we meet for lunch, we share problems and solutions—in complete confidence. We all feel pretty good after our discussions, which are open and free from judgement. In my younger days, I found it difficult to embrace a particular church or religious creed, despite the best intentions of those who tried to provide me with spiritual leadership. Like many, I came to realize that lessons in spiritual leadership are not always learned from those who profess to have it. Lessons abound, though, if you keep your heart open and your pride in check.

20

"Therefore, let thy words
be few."

ECCLESIASTES 4:2

Peace

AS WE GROW OLDER and life becomes a bit more burdensome,
our challenge is finding peace with ourselves in the third
act of our lives. We are no longer young athletes on the
basketball court or the driving force behind a bold business move. Our days as leaders are numbered, but unless
we are handicapped by mental or physical health problems,
how much do we hang on to and how much do we hand
over? Lessons in leadership in this area are more difficult to
find, or maybe they are just the ones we have to learn for
ourselves.

None of us can go back in time. We can only go forward,
but sometimes in a quiet moment, I think of myself setting
out from Edmonton in that yellow convertible in 1968. I
was thirty years old and determined to seek my fortune in
Vancouver. It was not the epic journey of an immigrant or
a refugee, but it was my journey and, to me, important. In

looking for lessons now, to lead me through this next phase of my life, I ask myself, "What would I trade if I could have the time back and repeat that journey? What would I trade for another fifty years?"

I would not trade Brenda—not for a century of centuries. Brenda has made my life complete. She is the kindest and most selfless person I know. She has a deep sense of herself and has worked hard on this area of her life. Early in our marriage, I was too headstrong and too busy to really listen to her. Fortunately, and through many tough experiences, I came to understand and appreciate the depth of her knowledge and insight. Brenda lost her mother when she was thirteen and it forever changed her view of life, but it did not diminish it. She radiates the joy of life and is full of goodness. For more than forty years, I have watched her interact with people from all walks of life. She is unimpressed by wealth, power, or ego. So much for all my efforts! She is impressed by kindness, humility, and grace. She is impressed by realism and hope. We have faced many challenges together and lived the vows we took on our wedding day. She is the best communicator I know and can read me like a book. Brenda keeps me centred but always in a loving and caring manner. She is the strength of our family.

I would not trade my two sons, Jason and Sacha—not for a million miles of track and a majority share in a railroad on Mars. Watching them come into their own as men, husbands, and fathers has been one of the great joys of my life. I never knew my brothers, but in the company of my sons, I think I've found them.

I would not trade my daughters-in-law, Melanie and A.J., who put up with all of my idiosyncrasies with patience and affection. Their intelligence is matched by a sense of adventure that will always keep my two sons hopping. Melanie is a naturopathic physician and A.J. is a talented broker in our real estate division. They are warm-hearted, funny, and wise. We are a family of volunteers with a bit of an addiction to public service but Melanie and A.J. are there for the dinners, the fundraisers, and the other community events we support, and when I see them enter a room, smiling and up for an evening of chicken and small talk, I am reminded of what it means to be truly engaged with your community.

I would not trade my grandchildren. I would not trade Hazel's steady look when she calls me Gaga instead of Grampa. I would not trade seeing Liam lick every chocolate cupcake on the dining room table before the rest of the guests are called in for the dessert buffet. I would not trade time spent with dear little Lucy, who arrived just this past summer and already shows signs of abundant charm. I would not trade the grandchildren I know now or the ones that are or may be on the way. I can't wait to meet them.

I would not trade a single Christmas, anniversary, or birthday celebration with my family, who accuse me every year of overspending and overcelebrating. I don't care. The rules about one present per family member don't apply to me. I believe in overcelebrating and intend to do so until the end. I did not get enough of it as a boy and I am making up for it now. My dog, Henry, and I often shop together because he is less critical about my tendency to excess. He waits in the car and I go into the store to retrieve the gifts. Afterwards, we go to the White Spot drive-through. I order for Henry, who sits in the passenger seat. He always gets a tray of his own.

"Two hamburgers, no buns, no sauce, relish, cheese, mustard, ketchup, pickles, or onions," I say. "And for me, a double-cheeseburger and a chocolate milkshake—no whipped cream. Hold the whipped cream."

No, I would not trade Henry for a trip back in time, unless he went with me. I love that dog, and I depend on him to write my annual Christmas letter.

I would not trade the lessons I learned from my early mentors—my scoutmaster, Henry White, and my law professors, Wilbur Fee Bowker and Dr. Alexander Smith. They are all gone now, but I learned lessons in leadership from each of them at a time in my life when the lessons stuck.

I would not trade hearing Coach Macintosh say "McLean you're in" on the night my east-end high school won the city basketball championship.

I would not trade knowing that my parents made a life for themselves and their children that started in a railway station house, and I would not trade the sound of trains coming and going in the night as I slept upstairs in that little house.

So as I look to the future and to the end of my many years as chairman of the CN board, I embrace and welcome the lessons that lie ahead. There are so many new things to enjoy and experience—my growing clan of grandchildren, my extended family, my good friends, business opportunities, travel, continued education, and maybe the odd lecture or speaking engagement where I can throw some light on the world from my perspective.

Freedom leads to destiny. We get the time given to us and we do the best we can with it. I am content with what

I have been given and what I have done. But if I could drive another hundred kilometres in that yellow convertible at the age of thirty—what would I trade?

I might trade some of my CN stock.

Or—maybe not.

Afterword

MY FATHER TURNED seventy a few years ago and I remember fretting about his birthday present. My first thought was to buy him a gong: a great big golden gong with a mallet for beating it. For, as my mother has said for years, the birthday boy is an absolute unmitigated Gong Show.

Then I thought about getting him an ear trumpet. You know the ones: those turn-of-the-century hearing aids made from horns in various shapes and sizes and exotic materials to be conspicuously held up to the ear with the head at a slight tilt, preferably while squinting. It would be the perfect gift to symbolize what some would say is a lifelong priority given to transmission over reception—and possibly finally tip the balance in reception's favour.

But I think what I finally settled on was a better fit. I recall a photo, now lost, of my father as a little boy greedily but lovingly devouring a melting ice cream cone. What a perfect metaphor for a life lived with passion and hunger—with the sweet promise of a jackpot just around the next corner—a life of a seeker whose work is never done. So I found for him the world's finest ice cream maker, an Italian job, naturally, so that he could make ice cream for his grandchildren while keeping a little back for himself for quality control purposes.

My dad looms large in our lives as a leader, as a moral reference point, and as someone to be teased with great care and diligence. As a child, I came to learn quickly that this teasing and testing, though seldom appreciated with outward displays of mirth on his face, was certainly appreciated by others around him—my mother most of all. So long as I avoided the nuclear ramifications of certain lines being crossed—such as playing in the sandbox while wearing my school uniform, volunteering to share details about my new Christmas presents with Canada Customs on a return trip from Hawaii, or not returning tools to their labelled place in the basement workshop—I inhabited the role of jester for much of my youth and some might say even a bit beyond. You can appreciate the irony when I ended up joining the family business.

You see, for Sacha and me, in our conception of our dad as boss, the true demonstration of his leadership—the real test of this type-A, force-of-nature, bull-in-a-china-shop guy—is *not* whether we respect his strength and creativity, his ability to deal with adversity, his entrepreneurship, the passion he brings to his endeavours, and the way he always finds the best in people. No, these things—undoubtedly great contributors to his business successes—do not in themselves tell the story of why the McLean Group of liberal capitalists works so well for the four of us. The true demonstration of David George Alexander McLean's leadership is the space he has created for us—his two sons—to develop our own sense of purpose, of responsibility, and our own leadership. Our dad, naturally under our mother's constant adult supervision, has created a work environment where we are permitted to make mistakes and encouraged to learn from them, to take our business interests to places he might not have chosen, and to continually evolve.

Many strong owner-founder business leaders could not possibly have had the openness, perspective, and humility required to create this environment. Sacha and I want nothing more out of our careers than to work together like this, wherever it takes us, and we are grateful for the opportunity. We know how lucky we are, and we intend to continue the journey.

It occurs to me in closing how difficult it is to write about one's father. Much about a relationship between father and son is necessarily implied, even codified, in a web of acknowledged but seldom talked about emotional entanglements. So I suppose a break with the male tradition of quiet acknowledgement of these things is in order—at least for one book.

Dad, you have been a wonderful father to Sacha and me. You are an inspiring leader and mentor. You have taught us so much about generosity, compassion, ambition, grit, and character. You care deeply about the people around you and remind us to be engaged with the world and all the communities we inhabit. You have been a joy to grow up with (well, most of the time), and Sacha and I love working with you. With Mom, you have built a marriage and a family of lasting closeness that your grandchildren will be lucky to share. So, Old Man, on the publication of this, your book of memories, thank you. You are much loved.

JASON MCLEAN
President and Chief Executive Officer
The McLean Group of Companies

Acknowledgements

WHEN I DECIDED to write this book I was encouraged by my family, with a note of caution from my wife, Brenda, who is always mindful of the privacy of others. She was right, of course. Telling a good and truthful story about my experiences in life, business, and at CN would need to be tempered with respect for what should and should not be said. Fortunately, I had good advisors. Some helped me write the book, some helped me in having something to write about, and some did a little of both. With that in mind, I would like to thank the following people.

To my co-writer, Patricia (Tricia) Finn, whose literary talent made this book so much better than anything I could have written on my own. Your wonderful sense of humour and creative spirit added emotional depth to my stories and structure in the telling of them. Your meticulous research and fact-checking have made the book much more readable and accurate, and I am very much in your debt.

To my friend Sean Finn (no relation to Tricia Finn), executive vice-president, corporate services, and chief legal officer at CN, who read the manuscript at my request and offered many helpful observations, all of which were positive. Sean, you are a very dear friend who has provided me with many years of advice and guidance at CN. I am forever grateful.

To Jonathan Burke, president and COO of Blackcomb Aviation, who generously gave of his time on short notice to read the manuscript at a stage when it was in danger of shifting off course. Your insightful comments inspired us to make some important adjustments.

To Darren Dahl, a senior associate dean at the Sauder School of Business, who gave up some of his summer vacation to read the manuscript. Your observations were astute and helpful in every way.

To my literary agent, Robert Mackwood, who assisted in getting this project into the capable hands of the publishing team at Greystone Books—Publisher Rob Sanders, Associate Publisher Nancy Flight, and Production Editor Shirarose Wilensky. You have been great partners.

WHEN IT COMES to my family business, there are many people to thank but I would like to make special mention of a few long-serving (some might say suffering) staff at McLean Group headquarters.

Thank you to Norm Elliot, executive vice-president, finance, for the McLean Group, whose professional attention to our family business made it so much easier for me to divide my time between a family business and CN.

Thank you to Kenny Diebel, senior vice-president, real estate, whose loyal and lengthy service is very much valued and appreciated by every member of my family.

Thank you to Dave Beck, a master of all construction trades and a key member of our diverse construction projects.

Thank you to Inga Buchanan, a trusted executive assistant who has kept me organized and productive for twenty-three years.

Thank you to Joan Hennen, who has been with me for forty years, transitioning from my shorthand-taking legal secretary to her recent appointment (on the occasion of her ninetieth birthday) as chief *education* officer (CEO) for the McLean Group. Joan, you grace us with your presence every Thursday when you arrive for work with your daughter Trudy, another important member of our staff. You correct our grammar and frown when we split our infinitives and misplace our modifiers. You are a wonder.

MY YEARS AT CN would not have been possible without a great many advisors, colleagues, and friends. Here are some of the people who have made my journey both possible and worthwhile.

To all of the members of the CN board of directors, past and present, thank you for teaching me the importance of patience and judgement in our deliberations. Our decisions were always made in the best interest of the company, and it has been a pleasure and privilege to work with all of you.

To Gerry Burgess, manager of administration at CN, who has set a high bar for service and professional dedication to CN. Gerry, thank you for your integrity and support. I appreciate everything you have done for me.

To Marie Andrée Vaillancourt, manager of board services at CN, whose attention to detail has made our board activities exceptional. Marie, you are a gem.

To Rudy Sita, CN guru of all things high tech, who has patiently dealt with all of us to ensure we are always properly connected.

To Marie France Bernier and more recently, Maria Karantabias, my valued Montreal assistants who have looked after me better than I deserved.

To my longtime friend Peter Jones, whose counsel over the years I so warmly appreciate. Peter, you have an exceptional talent of keeping your head when everyone else is losing theirs, and I thank you for your friendship and advice on so many occasions.

To Eddie Goldenberg, senior policy advisor to Prime Minister Chrétien, who was an important link with the Prime Minister's Office during the IPO. You were always available and always helpful, and if I did a better job, it was thanks to your counsel.

To Senator Ross Fitzpatrick, a wise confidant and friend for many years. Ross, I am deeply grateful to you for your loyalty and support.

To a friend for almost fifty years, the Right Honourable Jean Chrétien, former prime minister of Canada, thank you for all your support over the years. Your appointment of me to the board of CN was the impetus for all the events of the past twenty years at CN. I am so grateful to you for the confidence you have shown in me. You will always be the greatest prime minister this country has ever seen.

THANK YOU MOST of all, though, to my family—Brenda, Jason, Sacha, Melanie, Andrea, Hazel, Liam, Lucy, and the ones on the way. You are the stars of my universe. You keep me grounded, make me laugh, and help me see the important things in life.

Jason and Sacha, you have put up with a lot over the years, but you are always positive and supportive. I am blessed to have two such amazing sons. Your children—my beautiful grandchildren—provide me with hope for the future and I love them dearly.

Finally, to dear Brenda. It gives me the greatest pleasure just to be with you. You give me strength and encouragement, and your faith in "fearless communication" keeps our family strong. I constantly wonder how I was so fortunate to have found you some forty-four years ago. You are a beautiful person, and your wisdom and your love have made me a better man.

Index

NAFTA, 190
National Ethnic Coalition of
    Organizations, 233
Nesbitt Burns, 16, 168
Neufeld, Edward, 161
New York City, 84–85
Nixon, Richard, 247
Noranda Inc., 229
North American Life, 97
Northstar International Studios,
    114–115, 120
Nu-West Development
    Corporation, 102

O'Connor, James "Jim," 232–234
Odgers Berndtson, 130
Office of the Prime Minister of
    Canada, 135
Officer of the Order of Canada, 158,
    159, 160, 161, 229, 231, 232
oil and gas division, 211
oil spill, 202–203, 204–206
Olympic Games, 129
Omega Air Corporation, 127–128
One Canada (Diefenbaker), 24
Ontario Energy Savings Corp., 227
operating ratio (OR), 193
Order of Railroad Telegraphers, 21
Osgoode Hall Law School, 158
Ottawa apartment buildings, 94
Ottawa, Ontario and IPO, 155–162,
    166–170
Oxford University, 150

Pace Group, 157–158
Pace, Robert, 157–158, 234
Pacific Backlot Services, 123
Pacific Salmon Foundation, 205
Parker, Jackie, 56
Parker, Joe, 99
Pattison, Jimmy, 190
Peddie School, 227

Pemberton, B.C., 129
Penn, Ian, 242
pension funds, 15, 90, 184
Pershing Square Capital
    Management, 222
Petro-Canada, 171
Philips Electronics Canada,
    111–112
Phoenix, Arizona, 130
Phoenix Technology Services, 229
Pitcairn, James, 110
Placer Dome, 232
planned communities, 115–116
"plumb the depths," 245, 250
Porter Airlines, 232
power line construction, 129
prayer, 246, 248
Price Club, 113, 114
Price Waterhouse, 230
PricewaterhouseCoopers, 230
Prison Fellowship, 247
privatization, 143–149, 150, 152,
    154, 164, 169, 171, 185–186, 222
production facilities, 118–119,
    122–123
property values, 107
prostate cancer, 244–248
prostate-specific antigen
    (PSA), 250

Q badge, 45–46
Quebec referendum, 10, 178,
    181–182
Queen's University, 117, 231, 232

radiation, 250
railway mergers, 197
Rasmussen, Soren, 110, 112
RBC Dominion Securities, 167–168,
    169, 174
Reagan government, 99
real estate appraisers, 99

spiritual beliefs, 180, 242, 247
spiritual group, 244, 250–251
Spohn, Michael, 82
sports, 40
Squamish River, 204–206
Stanford University's Graduate School of Business, 131
Starrett City, 82
Steer, George, 65
Stembler, Anne, 86, 91
Stembler, Bill, 86, 91
Steuart Place, 99–100, 103
St. George's School, 42–43, 44–46, 145
Still Creek, 116, 123
Still Creek Village, 115–116, 119
Stimpson, Fred, 77, 82, 84, 87–88, 89–91
Stingray TV show, 118
stock, 10–11
Stone, Ruby, 74
Stornoway residence, 146
strategic planning committee, 191
stress, financial, 104–107
STRIKE, LABOUR, 163–164
   Montreal, Quebec, 164–165
   Ottawa, Ontario, 166–170
Studio Air Group, 126–127
succession planning, 133–140, 212
Surface Transportation Board (STB), 192–194, 197
Switzerland, 152–153

Talisman Energy Inc., 232
talking stick, 180–181
tax law, 99
tax treaties, 94
TD Bank Financial Group, 230
TD Securities, 168, 169
Teck Resources, 230

telecommunications, 92, 123
Teleglobe, 230
telegraphers, 21
television production, 92.
   see also film industry
TELLIER, PAUL
   board meeting, 194–197
   bonus, 187–188
   Canadian Pacific Railway, 190–191
   as CEO, 14–15, 149–152, 210–213
   CN's financial performance, 189
   communication, 194–196
   Hilton Hotel meeting, 182–183
   Illinois Central, 190–193
   IPO preparations, 154–155
   share allocation, 182
   strike strategy, 164–165
   talking stick, 180–181
   trip out west, 177–178
Telus, 231
tenants, 117–118
Tercek, Mark, 15, 173
375 Water Street, 97
Toronto-Dominion Bank, 231
Toronto, Ontario, 82–83
TransAlta Corporation, 227
Trudeau, Pierre Elliott, 16, 144–145, 157, 229
Tryton Investment Co. Ltd., 160
Turner, John, 16
21 Jump Street TV show, 118
Twigg-Smith family, 100, 103
Twigg-Smith, Thurston, 100
Twin Mining Corporation, 229

unions, labour, 163–165
UNITED STATES
   Class 1 railway mergers, 197

DAVID MCLEAN, O.B.C., LL.D., F.ICD., is chairman of the McLean Group, a family business active in real estate investment, film production services, and aviation. He is an outspoken champion of entrepreneurship, education, and community service. Mr. McLean has chaired many boards, including CN, Coastland Wood Industries, Concord Pacific Group, the Vancouver Board of Trade, the Canadian Chamber of Commerce, and the Board of Governors at the University of British Columbia. David McLean was born in Calgary and received his law degree from the University of Alberta. He lives in Vancouver with his wife, Brenda, vice-chair of the McLean Group, and their beloved dog, Henry. The McLeans have two sons, Jason and Sacha, who provide refreshing second-generation leadership to the family business.

PATRICIA FINN is a professional writer and editor. Born in Winnipeg, she was educated in Canada and New Zealand, where she studied English, classics, and music. She is an established film and television writer, a member of the Writers Guild of Canada, and the director of communications for the McLean Group. She lives in Vancouver.